PLANT-PROTEIN RECIPES
That You'll Love

Enjoy the Goodness and Deliciousness of 150+ Healthy Plant-Protein Recipes!

CARINA WOLFF

Adams Media

New York   London   Toronto   Sydney   New Delhi

Adams Media
An Imprint of Simon & Schuster, Inc.
57 Littlefield Street
Avon, Massachusetts 02322

First Adams Media hardcover edition DECEMBER 2017

ADAMS MEDIA and colophon are trademarks of Simon and Schuster.

For information about special discounts for bulk purchases, please contact Simon & Schuster Special Sales at 1-866-506-1949 or business@simonandschuster.com.

The Simon & Schuster Speakers Bureau can bring authors to your live event. For more information or to book an event contact the Simon & Schuster Speakers Bureau at 1-866-248-3049 or visit our website at www.simonspeakers.com.

Interior design by Heather McKiel
Interior photographs by Carina Wolff
Author photograph by Natalie Wentworth

Manufactured in the United States of America

10 9 8 7 6 5 4 3 2 1

Library of Congress Cataloging-in-Publication Data has been applied for.

ISBN 978-1-5072-0452-8
ISBN 978-1-5072-0453-5 (ebook)

Always follow safety and commonsense cooking protocols while using kitchen utensils, operating ovens and stoves, and handling uncooked food. If children are assisting in the preparation of any recipe, they should always be supervised by an adult.

Dedication

This book is dedicated to the memory of my uncle Claude, who I love and miss so much.

Contents

7. SIDE DISHES 139

8. DINNER ENTRÉES 161

Introduction

Anyone who follows a plant-based diet knows that the most common question people ask is "How do you get your protein?" When people think of protein, their mind usually goes to steak or chicken dinners, and they somehow can't fathom that a plant-based diet could provide an adequate amount of the nutrient. However, even though animal products might be the first sources of protein that come to mind, they aren't the only ones available.

Plenty of plant-based products such as beans, oats, and nuts are loaded with protein, and with the proper food combinations found in the 150-plus recipes in this book, you can make vegetarian meals that are just as balanced and satisfying as their meat-filled counterparts. So if you're sick of eating the same old dishes filled with the same ingredients, *Plant-Protein Recipes That You'll Love* will help you ditch your boring routine and open the door to exciting, delicious, protein-filled meals, from Vegetable Tofu Scramble to Black Bean Enchilada Bake and Barbecue Tempeh Pizza to White Bean Blondies. All of these dishes not only taste great, but they provide you with all the protein you need to stay healthy.

While you may have heard about people investing in pricey protein supplements or buying outrageously priced obscure ingredients from the health food store, plant-based dishes don't have to be expensive. Here you'll find recipes for every meal ranging from breakfast to dinner to dessert, and every one of them is packed with everyday vegetables, grains, nuts, and seeds that are protein-filled and delicious. And if you do decide you want to use protein powders, you'll find a few recipes for different powders you can make at home instead of spending your hard-earned money on store-bought ones. Simply add these to anything from your smoothies or pancake mix to your pasta sauces when you need an extra boost. These powders make a great option when you're in a rush or you've spent a lot of time working out and need additional protein. If you're short on time and aren't able to whip up a full meal, you can throw these powders in a blender and have a protein-rich drink ready in just minutes. This can be especially useful if your protein needs are higher from working out, as you can enjoy something like a smoothie with your regular meal, or you can make a nutrient-dense drink using whole plant-foods and your protein powder as a supplement.

This book will help you understand the best food combinations to provide you with proper nutrition—but without slaving away in the kitchen or breaking the bank. Hopefully, the recipes in this book will also inspire you to come up with your own unique, protein-filled plant-based dishes.

Incorporating more plant-based foods into your diet can be intimidating. But whether you're someone who follows a vegetarian diet or you're just trying to adapt more Meatless Mondays into your life, once you start playing around in the kitchen and see how many different foods actually provide a good amount of protein, you'll start to realize it's not as daunting as it sounds. You might even find that your Meatless Mondays extend on even later into the week.

CHAPTER 1

WHAT YOU NEED TO KNOW ABOUT PLANT-BASED PROTEINS

Before you start cooking with plant-based proteins, you'll want to know everything there is to know about what they are and why you should be using them. In this chapter, you'll learn it all—from why you should be eating plant-based proteins instead of always eating meat to the many health benefits plant-based proteins provide to the money you'll save on changing up your diet. You'll even discover some unexpected foods that contain protein. You'll also be armed with information on how you can make your own protein powders at home, for those days when you just don't feel like eating any more beans and lentils.

Whether you're a beginner just switching to more meatless meals or whether you've been eating vegetarian foods forever, in this chapter you'll learn all the information you could need to start incorporating even more plant-based, protein-filled meals into your life.

What *Are* Plant-Based Proteins?

First, let's talk about what plant proteins are and how much of them you should be eating. Protein is an important building block in your body, as it is essential for creating everything from bones, to muscles, to the tissue in our organs. You need protein to repair cells and make new ones; to build muscle; to have healthy hair, skin, and nails; and to make enzymes, hormones, and other chemicals. Plant-based proteins are protein sources that come from plants. "Plants" include everything from vegetables (such as spinach or corn), to legumes (such as peanuts or lentils), nuts (such as almonds or walnuts), and seeds (such as

quinoa or hemp), to whole grains (such as oats or rice). As long as the protein isn't derived from an animal—so no meat or poultry, dairy, or eggs—it's considered a plant protein.

As far as how much protein each person needs per day, it differs depending on factors such as sex, weight, activity level, etc. The recommended dietary allowance (RDA) for protein is 0.8 grams per kilogram (about 2.2 pounds) of body weight. You can calculate the amount of protein you need by multiplying your weight in pounds by 0.36. For an average adult male, that ends up being 56 grams of protein a day. For an average female, it comes out to around 46 grams a day. However, if you train or exercise a lot, you may require more protein. If you're curious about how much protein is ideal for your body and lifestyle, it's best to speak to a doctor or nutritionist who can best evaluate your needs.

Benefits of Plant-Based Proteins

If you're just starting to experiment with plant-based proteins, you may find yourself wondering, "Why make the switch?" Let's take a look at the benefits:

They Help with Weight Loss

Many people switch to plant-based diets to lose weight, and research supports that decision. A 2016 study from the *Journal of General Internal Medicine* found that following a vegan or vegetarian diet is the most effective for weight loss compared to other common, popular diets that are non-vegetarian. In general, protein is good for losing weight because it helps keep you fuller for longer, but plant-based proteins are even better because they don't contain as much saturated fat or as many calories as animal products.

They're Healthier

Although it can seem more convenient, relying too much on animal products for protein can come with some negative health effects including a higher risk of heart disease, type 2 diabetes, and cancer. Additionally, consuming a large amount of meat and poultry can mean getting too much protein, which can increase your risk of kidney disease, cardiovascular disease, and certain cancers. For example, animal protein tends to have a higher proportion of the essential amino acids, which results in a higher production of the hormone insulin-like growth factor-1 (IGF-1). This hormone has been linked with increased cancer risk. Another risk with too much animal protein is that it is abundant in heme iron. Althogh heme iron is a necessary nutrient, too much of it can cause oxidative stress and free-radical damage.

Although there's no exact breakdown of how much animal protein you should be eating, it's best to keep your meals balanced and your protein sources as varied as possible. It's also best to avoid going too much over the RDA for protein, especially if you're only eating meat.

By choosing to eat more plant-based proteins, you help lower your risk of these diseases, especially because plant-based foods contain many beneficial phytonutrients—natural chemicals that help prevent disease, strengthen your immune system, fight aging, and more.

In addition, switching to a plant-based diet can help you eat more whole, unprocessed foods, which can help you avoid the additives and preservatives found in certain meat and poultry products. Some manufacturers of animal-based products include additives and preservatives to make the products last longer, to boost their color, or to add moisture and flavor. However, the safety of their use is unclear, as different studies show different results. Some research has found that these additives could be carcinogenic or cause a number of other health problems.

They're Kind to the Environment

In addition to the positive health effects, switching to plant-based foods also has a positive impact on the environment. Livestock production is responsible for a significant portion of greenhouse gas emissions, so cutting down on meat consumption can help reduce our carbon footprint. It also takes a hundred times more water to produce a pound of animal protein than a pound of grain protein, which makes plant-based proteins much more efficient for preserving water on our planet.

They Save You Money

Eating a diet rich in plant proteins might even end up being easier on your wallet, as plant-based foods tend to be less expensive than meat, poultry, or fish. For example, a bag of dried beans or lentils is much cheaper than a steak. Lentils cost about 1.6 cents per gram of protein, while steak costs 4.5 cents per gram of protein. Buying these products in bulk can help cut down on costs and can last for months, which means you won't have to throw any leftovers away.

Protein-Packed Plants

You know what plant-based proteins are and why you should use them, so let's take a look at the best places to find this protein. After all, understanding which plant-based foods are high in protein can help you put together unique and delicious meals that provide you with the nutrients you need to stay healthy and balanced. Almost all of these foods are available at your local grocery store, so you won't have to run around town looking for any specialty ingredients.

Beans

- Black beans: 15 grams protein per 1 cup cooked
- White beans: 15 grams protein per 1 cup cooked
- Kidney beans: 15 grams protein per 1 cup cooked
- Lima beans: 15 grams protein per 1 cup cooked
- Pinto beans: 15 grams protein per 1 cup cooked

Grains

- Barley: 3.5 grams protein per 1 cup cooked
- Oats: 6 grams protein per 1 cup cooked
- Brown rice: 5 grams protein per 1 cup cooked
- Wild rice: 7 grams protein per 1 cup cooked

Greens

- Broccoli: 2.5 grams protein per 1 cup chopped broccoli
- Kale: 3 grams protein per 1 cup chopped kale leaves
- Spinach: 1 gram protein per 1 cup spinach leaves

Legumes

- Chickpeas: 15 grams protein per 1 cup cooked
- Edamame: 17 grams protein per 1 cup cooked
- Peanuts: 7 grams protein per 1 ounce
- Tempeh: 31 grams protein per 1 cup
- Tofu: 20 grams protein per 1 cup
- Lentils: 18 grams protein per 1 cup cooked

Nuts

- Almonds: 6 grams protein per 1 ounce
- Cashews: 5 grams protein per 1 ounce
- Walnuts: 4.3 grams protein per 1 ounce
- Pistachios: 6 grams protein per 1 ounce

Seeds

- Chia seeds: 4.7 grams protein per 1 ounce
- Flaxseeds: 5.2 grams protein per 1 ounce
- Hemp seeds: 9.2 grams protein per 1 ounce
- Pumpkin seeds: 5 grams protein per 1 ounce
- Sesame seeds: 5 grams protein per 1 ounce
- Sunflower seeds: 6 grams protein per 1 ounce
- Quinoa: 8 grams protein per 1 cup cooked

Vegetables

- Artichokes: 4.2 grams protein per 1 medium artichoke
- Brussels sprouts: 3 grams protein per 1 cup
- Corn: 5 grams protein per 1 cup cooked
- Peas: 9 grams protein per 1 cup cooked
- Potatoes: 4.3 grams protein per 1 medium potato
- Sweet potatoes: 2 grams protein per 1 medium sweet potato

Other

- Nutritional yeast: 3 grams protein per 1 tablespoon

Combining these different plant-based foods can help ensure you get the protein content you desire. It's also good to switch up how you get your protein. Some meals might be more soy-based, while others might contain more greens. By alternating food groups, you maximize the amount of nutrients you get in your meals while still getting in your protein.

Protein Powders

Protein powders are used to supplement your diet with more protein in a concentrated form. They are a blend of different protein sources that can be used in drinks like smoothies and shakes or even added to your meals for an extra boost of protein. Many store-bought protein powders contain animal-based ingredients such as whey and casein, but there are many plant-based options available. However, you can also make your own plant-based protein powders at home, which can be a great way to add more protein to meals

that are lacking or to regular food and drinks that don't typically contain any protein.

Protein Powders versus Whole Foods

For many people, using protein powder is a convenient way to load up on the nutrient. But are you missing out when using a powder instead of eating a whole food?

On the one hand, you can get a lot of protein without consuming a lot of calories when using a protein powder, and it's useful to add to certain meals that need a little boost. However, protein powders lack the wider variety of nutrients you get when eating whole foods, especially if you're only drinking something like a shake. Although a drink may contain some healthy ingredients and the protein you need, the wider the variety of vegetables and other plant sources you use, the more vitamins, minerals, and other nutrients you get in the meal. A shake may contain a good amount of protein, but you'll want to alternate eating fruit and powder-based protein drinks with whole foods like salad, which have a wider variety of nutrients. Therefore, it's important to try to eat whole foods as much as you can and utilize protein powders when you need a boost or if you don't have time to whip up a full meal.

How to Cook with Plant-Based Protein Powders

Protein powders are most commonly used in smoothies and shakes, but there are a variety of other ways you can incorporate them into your everyday recipes:

- Add them to your coffee.
- Mix them into pancake and waffle batter.
- Stir them into soup broth.
- Cook them in your oatmeal.
- Mix them into pasta sauce.
- Add them to your veggie burger patties.
- Stir them into dressing.
- Mix them into chia seed pudding.
- Add them to your cookie or muffin batter.
- Sprinkle them on your morning toast.

Keep in mind that your recipe should never be more than 50 percent protein powder, or your food can end up tasting dry and chalky. That said, feel free to experiment with different amounts depending on the recipe. For example, something like a smoothie can handle a whole serving (¼ cup) of protein powder, but if you're adding some to a pasta sauce, you might want to start with a smaller amount. The more you experiment, the more comfortable you'll get and the more easily you'll be able to incorporate different powders into your everyday meals.

Make Your Own Protein Powder

Many people like to use protein powder in their cooking, but the problem with many commercial protein powders is that they often contain unnecessary additives or unwanted ingredients such as dairy or refined sugar. Therefore, making your own protein powder at home is a great solution because you get to control exactly what goes inside of it. Plus, protein powders tend to be expensive, so this can help you save some money.

There are a few different ways you can make your own protein powders at home. The first is using ingredients you already have in your cabinet, such as seeds, nuts, and grains, and blending them into a fine powder. This is a quick and convenient way to make a protein mix to add to your food.

Another way to make your own protein powder is by creating your own special blends using plant-protein powders that contain concentrated amounts of protein, such as brown rice powder or pea protein powder. These powders are more than just blended dried peas or brown rice in powder form, so unfortunately they're not able to be made at home. Pea protein powder is made by extracting the soluble pea protein from yellow split peas. It's the same process for brown rice, just extracted from brown rice. This is what causes the powder to have a high concentration of protein compared to just grounding up dried peas or rice at home.

Pea protein and brown rice protein are available in health food stores, vitamin shops, or on Amazon, and you can use them to make your own unique powder blends. Although you may have to go a bit out of your way to get them, they give you the most bang for your buck, as they contain the highest amount of protein compared to other nuts or seeds you may have at home. Plus, they are cheaper than buying a premade protein powder.

If it's easier for you to make your own protein powder using ingredients you already have, great. But just keep in mind that the protein count per serving is going to be significantly lower than if you use brown rice protein or pea protein. It's nice to be able to make both depending on what type of meals you'll be using them for.

You can experiment with protein powder blends of your own, but I've provided three recipes to serve all your different needs. The first powder is one you can make completely from scratch. The second is a powder made with brown rice protein powder. The third is one made from pea powder. You can adjust these to make them savory or sweet by adding or subtracting ingredients such as stevia, vanilla powder, cocoa powder, garlic powder, onion powder, and more.

These three homemade protein-powder recipes can be found on the following pages.

"From Scratch" Protein Powder

This protein powder recipe uses different types of seeds that are ground up and mixed together. You can find all these seeds at your regular grocery store. This protein powder works best in heartier foods such as baked goods, soups, or sauces.

Makes 8 (¼ cup) servings

Recipe Prep Time: *5 minutes*
Recipe Cook Time: *N/A*

¾ cup chia seeds
¾ cup raw unsalted sunflower seeds
¾ cup hemp seeds
¾ cup flaxseed meal

Grind together all ingredients in a food processor or blender on high until a fine powder has formed, about 10–20 seconds. Store in a lidded jar or other airtight container in a cool, dry place. Protein powder will keep for a few weeks.

Per Serving

Calories: 282 | Fat: 20.5 g | Protein: 12.6 g | Sodium: 2 mg
Fiber: 9.2 g | Carbohydrates: 12.2 g | Sugar: 0.3 g

Chocolate Cinnamon Brown Rice Protein Powder

This sweet protein powder works well in smoothies, desserts, and breakfast foods. If you don't want the powder to be sweet, just remove the cocoa, cinnamon, and stevia. For something more savory, you can replace the cinnamon with garlic powder.

Makes 8 (¼ cup) servings

Recipe Prep Time: *5 minutes*
Recipe Cook Time: *N/A*

1½ cups raw sliced almonds
1½ cups brown rice protein powder
2 tablespoons unsweetened cocoa powder
1 tablespoon ground cinnamon
2 teaspoons stevia extract powder

1 In a food processor or blender on high speed, grind almonds until a fine powder has formed, about 10–15 seconds.
2 Add protein powder, cocoa, cinnamon, and stevia, and blend until mixed. Store in a lidded jar or other airtight container in a cool, dry place. Protein powder will keep for a few weeks.

Per Serving

Calories: 137 | Fat: 10.7 g | Protein: 7.4 g | Sodium: 7 mg
Fiber: 3.4 g | Carbohydrates: 6.5 g | Sugar: 0.8 g

Ginger Pea Protein Powder

This protein powder contains a mix of pea protein powder and flaxseed meal, and it's flavored with some ground ginger and stevia extract powder. This powder works well for smoothies, baked goods, desserts, and breakfast foods. If you want to use it for savory foods, just remove the stevia. Pea protein powder tends to have the strongest taste of the protein powders, so just be aware of this when using it in foods and smoothies. You can always use less if the taste is too much to handle.

Makes 8 (¼ cup) servings

Recipe Prep Time: *5 minutes*
Recipe Cook Time: *N/A*

1½ cups pea protein powder
¾ cup flaxseed meal
2 tablespoons ground ginger
1½ teaspoons stevia extract
    powder

Mix together all ingredients in a small bowl. Store in a lidded jar or other airtight container in a cool, dry place. Protein powder will keep for a few weeks.

Per Serving

Calories: 211 | Fat: 5.2 g | Protein: 26.4 g | Sodium: 10 mg
Fiber: 3.4 g | Carbohydrates: 6.0 g | Sugar: 0.0 g

CHAPTER 2

BREAKFAST

Loaded White Bean Avocado Toast

You've likely seen avocado toast all over social media and may have been tempted to make it as a breakfast of your own. This recipe gives your toast a protein-filled boost by mixing in some white beans with the avocado. You can barely taste the beans, but they'll make your meal more nutritious and filling.

Serves 2

Recipe Prep Time: *10 minutes*
Recipe Cook Time: *N/A*

2 thin slices multigrain sourdough bread

¾ cup cooked or canned cannellini beans, rinsed and drained

1 medium ripe avocado, peeled and pitted

Juice of 2 small lemons

¼ cup assorted microgreens

2 tablespoons hemp seeds

½ teaspoon red pepper flakes

1 Toast bread until golden and crispy.

2 Add beans to a medium bowl and mash with a fork to make a paste. Add avocado and mash with a fork, folding avocado chunks into beans. Mix in lemon juice.

3 Spread the mixture evenly on the toast, and top with microgreens, hemp seeds, and red pepper flakes. Serve immediately.

Per Serving

Calories: 453 | Fat: 15.4 g | Protein: 18.7 g | Sodium: 423 mg
Fiber: 11.3 g | Carbohydrates: 60.0 g | Sugar: 4.7 g

··

WHY MICROGREENS?

You can top off your avocado toast with regular greens like kale and arugula, but microgreens not only fit nicely on the toast and provide a unique texture, but they contain 40 times more nutrients than greens that have fully matured.

··

Savory Breakfast Quinoa Bowl

Quinoa doesn't have to be just for lunch or dinner—it's an excellent protein source that can be eaten for breakfast as well. In this Savory Breakfast Quinoa Bowl, quinoa is mixed with tofu and spinach and topped off with avocado, sun-dried tomatoes, and feta cheese. All these amazing flavors combine to give you a California-inspired bowl that will satisfy all your savory cravings.

Serves 2

Recipe Prep Time: *5 minutes*
Recipe Cook Time: *20 minutes*

½ cup uncooked quinoa, rinsed well and drained

1 cup water

8 ounces firm organic tofu

1 tablespoon extra-virgin olive oil

3 cups whole spinach leaves

½ medium avocado, peeled and diced

⅓ cup chopped oil-packed sun-dried tomatoes

2 tablespoons crumbled feta cheese

Juice of 1 small lemon

¼ teaspoon black pepper

1 Add quinoa and water to a medium saucepan; bring to a boil over medium-high heat. Reduce to a simmer, cover, and cook until all water is absorbed, about 10–15 minutes.

2 Drain tofu and pat dry with paper towels. Add to a small bowl and mash with a fork until crumbly; set aside. Heat oil in a large saucepan over medium heat. Add spinach and sauté about 2 minutes until wilted. Lower heat to medium-low and add tofu. Cook about 1 minute until heated through. Mix in quinoa.

3 Transfer to a medium bowl and top with avocado, tomatoes, feta, lemon juice, and pepper. Serve warm.

Per Serving

Calories: 426 | Fat: 22.3 g | Protein: 19.6 g | Sodium: 192 mg
Fiber: 8.5 g | Carbohydrates: 39.1 g | Sugar: 1.6 g

Breakfast Quinoa with Blueberries and Peanut Butter

If you're sick of eating oatmeal or cereal for breakfast, try making some sweet quinoa instead. Quinoa tastes delicious when paired with almond milk, various nut butters, and whatever fruit is in season, so don't be afraid to change up the ingredients and personalize this protein-filled dish. If you need a little sweetener, drizzle a tiny bit of pure maple syrup over this dish.

Serves 2

Recipe Prep Time: *5 minutes*
Recipe Cook Time: *20 minutes*

½ cup uncooked quinoa

1 cup water

2 tablespoons unsalted raw creamy peanut butter

½ cup fresh blueberries

¼ teaspoon ground cinnamon

½ cup unsweetened almond milk

1 Add quinoa and water to a medium saucepan; bring to a boil over medium-high heat. Reduce to a simmer, cover, and cook until all water is absorbed, about 10–15 minutes.

2 Transfer quinoa to a medium bowl. Add peanut butter and blueberries on top, and finish off with cinnamon and almond milk. Serve immediately.

Per Serving

Calories: 280 | Fat: 11.1 g | Protein: 10.5 g | Sodium: 46 mg
Fiber: 5.5 g | Carbohydrates: 36.4 g | Sugar: 4.7 g

Vegetable Tofu Scramble

Whether you like to eat scrambled eggs for breakfast or you're just trying to get in your share of vegetables at the start of the day, you'll love this scramble. In this recipe, mashed tofu is a great substitution for scrambled eggs. It has a similar texture and consistency, and it's just as filling. Plus, you can load it up with all your favorite toppings and make this dish your own.

Serves 2

Recipe Prep Time: *10 minutes*
Recipe Cook Time: *10 minutes*

- 8 ounces organic extra-firm tofu
- 1 tablespoon extra-virgin olive oil
- 2 medium cloves garlic, peeled and finely chopped
- ½ cup peeled and chopped yellow onion
- 1¼ cups sliced button mushrooms
- 2 cups fresh baby spinach leaves
- ½ cup quartered cherry tomatoes
- ½ teaspoon turmeric powder
- ¼ teaspoon salt
- ½ teaspoon black pepper

1 Drain all liquid from tofu and place between paper towels to soak up any excess moisture. Let it sit about 5 minutes, then transfer to a medium bowl. Break up with a fork until crumbled.

2 Heat oil in a medium skillet over medium-low heat. Add garlic and cook 1 minute, stirring so it doesn't burn. Add onions and mushrooms; cook 4–5 minutes until onions are translucent and mushrooms begin to soften, stirring occasionally. Add spinach and cook about 2 minutes or until spinach begins to wilt.

3 Add cherry tomatoes, tofu, and turmeric; stir about 1 minute until tofu is heated through and all ingredients are evenly mixed. Season with salt and pepper. Serve warm.

Per Serving

Calories: 208 | Fat: 13.0 g | Protein: 14.5 g | Sodium: 328 mg
Fiber: 3.1 g | Carbohydrates: 11.8 g | Sugar: 4.3 g

ALWAYS OPT FOR ORGANIC TOFU

More than 90 percent of soy is genetically modified, so whenever you buy tofu, make sure to get organic. Research is mixed on GMOs, but better safe than sorry!

Cinnamon Roll Overnight Oats

Oats are a good source of plant-based protein, but it's tough to find time in the morning to cook yourself a bowl of oatmeal. If that sounds like you, these overnight oats are a great solution. It takes just 5 minutes to throw together the ingredients the night before, and by the morning, you'll have ready-to-eat oats that are nice and soft!

Serves 1

Recipe Prep Time: *6 hours*
Recipe Cook Time: *N/A*

½ cup unsweetened almond milk

1 tablespoon chia seeds

2 tablespoons raw almond butter

1 tablespoon pure maple syrup

¼ teaspoon ground cinnamon

¼ teaspoon pure vanilla extract

½ cup rolled oats

¾ tablespoon raw sliced almonds

1 In a small jar or bowl, mix together almond milk, chia seeds, almond butter, maple syrup, cinnamon, and vanilla until combined.

2 Add oats and stir until completely submerged in almond milk. Make sure to press down with a spoon so all the oats are covered.

3 Cover with a lid or plastic wrap and refrigerate at least 6 hours or overnight.

4 In the morning, top with almonds and eat chilled.

Per Serving

Calories: 479 | Fat: 26.0 g | Protein: 15.4 g | Sodium: 84 mg
Fiber: 12.3 g | Carbohydrates: 52.4 g | Sugar: 15.4 g

Peanut Butter Cup Oatmeal

You're not supposed to have candy for breakfast, but this oatmeal is the next best thing. This creamy combination of chocolate and peanut butter tastes like it should be dessert, but it's loaded with fiber and protein to help start off your day on the right note. And, since this dish is sweetened with just a little bit of maple syrup and doesn't include any refined sugar, you don't even have to feel guilty about feeding that sweet tooth.

Serves 1

Recipe Prep Time: *15 minutes*
Recipe Cook Time: *5 minutes*

½ cup water
½ cup unsweetened almond milk
½ cup rolled oats
2 tablespoons raw creamy peanut butter
1 tablespoon unsweetened cocoa powder
1½ teaspoons pure maple syrup

1 Add water and almond milk to a medium saucepan and bring to a boil over medium-high heat. Add oats and reduce to a simmer. Cover and cook 3–5 minutes until oats are soft.

2 Remove from heat and mix in peanut butter, cocoa powder, and maple syrup until evenly combined. Serve warm.

Per Serving

Calories: 392 | Fat: 21.0 g | Protein: 14.6 g | Sodium: 86 mg
Fiber: 9.0 g | Carbohydrates: 43.7 g | Sugar: 9.1 g

Savory Chickpea Oatmeal with Garlic Yogurt Sauce

When most people think of oatmeal, they think sweet, but just like any other grain, oatmeal can be prepared as a savory dish as well. The roasted chickpeas in this dish provide a hit of extra plant-based protein, and the soft sweetness of the tomatoes balances out the crispness of the chickpeas. The garlic yogurt sauce adds some extra creaminess, but if you're vegan, don't worry. This dish is delicious enough without it.

Serves 2

Recipe Prep Time: *5 minutes*
Recipe Cook Time: *20 minutes*

- 1 cup cooked or canned chickpeas
- 1 cup halved cherry tomatoes
- 1 tablespoon plus 1 teaspoon extra-virgin olive oil, divided
- 1 cup steel-cut oats
- ½ cup 2% plain Greek yogurt
- ¼ teaspoon garlic powder
- ¼ teaspoon paprika
- ½ small avocado, peeled and sliced
- ⅛ teaspoon salt
- ¼ teaspoon black pepper

1 Preheat oven to 425°F.

2 Pat chickpeas dry with a paper towel (removing the excess moisture before baking will help make them crispy). Line a medium baking sheet with aluminum foil.

3 Spread out chickpeas and tomatoes evenly on the prepared baking sheet; drizzle with 1 tablespoon oil. Bake 20 minutes until chickpeas are golden and crispy.

4 While chickpeas and tomatoes are roasting, prepare oatmeal according to package directions.

5 In a small bowl, combine yogurt, garlic powder, and paprika until smooth.

6 When oatmeal is ready, add to a serving bowl and top with roasted chickpeas and tomatoes, avocado, prepared yogurt sauce, remaining 1 teaspoon olive oil, salt, and black pepper. Serve warm.

Per Serving

Calories: 410 | Fat: 17.1 g | Protein: 17.0 g | Sodium: 336 mg
Fiber: 11.3 g | Carbohydrates: 47.7 g | Sugar: 7.9 g

Banana Honey Pancakes

These protein-filled banana pancakes don't contain any dairy, and the only sweetener used is honey. They taste great with a drizzle of maple syrup or even just some ghee, but to get an extra protein boost, you can top them with protein-rich foods such as walnuts, chia seeds, almond butter, or anything else that will start off your morning on the right foot.

Serves 4 (2 medium pancakes per serving)

Recipe Prep Time: *15 minutes*
Recipe Cook Time: *6 minutes*

1 medium ripe banana, peeled and mashed

1 cup unsweetened almond milk

1 teaspoon pure vanilla extract

¼ cup raw wild honey

1 cup whole-wheat flour

½ cup "From Scratch" Protein Powder (Chapter 1)

¼ teaspoon ground cinnamon

1½ teaspoons baking powder

1½ tablespoons coconut oil, divided

1 In a large bowl, combine banana, almond milk, vanilla, and honey until smooth.

2 In a medium bowl, combine flour, protein powder, cinnamon, and baking powder. Fold the dry ingredients into the wet ingredients until just combined (don't overmix to ensure your pancakes come out light and fluffy).

3 In a large skillet, heat ½ tablespoon coconut oil on medium. Add the batter to the pan using about ¼ cup batter per pancake. Cook about 2–3 minutes on each side, flipping when bubbly on top and the edges begin to firm up. Repeat until all batter is gone and you've made 8 medium pancakes, adding coconut oil to the pan as needed. Serve warm.

Per 1 Pancake

Calories: 374 | Fat: 14.8 g | Protein: 11.0 g | Sodium: 224 mg
Fiber: 8.6 g | Carbohydrates: 52.2 g | Sugar: 21.0 g

Strawberry Banana Almond Butter Toast

If you're a fan of peanut butter and jelly sandwiches, you'll love this breakfast toast. The almond butter is a nice change from the standard peanut butter, and the banana and strawberry slices add a sweet and juicy touch. Chia seeds are added for extra crunch as well as protein. With this fiber-filled breakfast, you definitely won't go hungry until lunch!

Serves 2

Recipe Prep Time: *10 minutes*
Recipe Cook Time: *N/A*

- 2 thin slices whole-grain bread
- 4 tablespoons raw almond butter, divided
- 1 medium banana, peeled and thinly sliced, divided
- 4 medium strawberries, trimmed and thinly sliced, divided
- 1 tablespoon chia seeds, divided
- ¼ teaspoon ground cinnamon, divided

1 Toast bread until golden and crispy. Spread 2 tablespoons almond butter on each slice. Top each slice with half the bananas and half the strawberries.

2 Sprinkle ½ tablespoon chia seeds and ⅛ teaspoon cinnamon on top of each toast. Serve immediately.

Per Serving

Calories: 345 | Fat: 18.7 g | Protein: 12.7 g | Sodium: 146 mg
Fiber: 9.8 g | Carbohydrates: 37.4 g | Sugar: 11.8 g

Baked Breakfast Sweet Potato

This meal is perfect for those who are on a gluten-free diet. While this recipe calls for only sunflower seeds, feel free to get creative with your nuts and seeds for additional protein. You can get creative with your cooking methods as well. Baking the sweet potato gives it the best flavor, but sticking it in the microwave for 3–4 minutes works too, especially on busy mornings.

Serves 1

Recipe Prep Time: *2 minutes*
Recipe Cook Time: *45 minutes*

1 medium sweet potato
1 tablespoon raw crunchy
   almond butter
2 tablespoons raw unsalted
   sunflower seeds
1 tablespoon chia seeds
¼ teaspoon ground
   cinnamon
½ teaspoon pure maple
   syrup

1 Preheat oven to 400°F. Line a medium baking sheet with aluminum foil.

2 Pierce sweet potato with a fork and place on the prepared baking sheet. Bake 40–45 minutes or until easily pierced with a fork.

3 Cut sweet potato in half lengthwise; spread almond butter on each side. Top with sunflower seeds, chia seeds, cinnamon, and maple syrup. Serve warm.

Per Serving

Calories: 351 | Fat: 18.8 g | Protein: 10.4 g | Sodium: 72 mg
Fiber: 11.4 g | Carbohydrates: 39.9 g | Sugar: 8.9 g

Cinnamon Coconut Granola

Granola has long been touted as a health food, but you may not realize that store-bought granola is often filled with refined sugar and refined grains, making it more of a junk food. Making your own granola at home, however, is a great way to make sure you're using all the right ingredients so you can enjoy your breakfast in peace. Serve this granola on top of Greek yogurt with berries or with almond milk as a cereal.

Serves 8

Recipe Prep Time: *25 minutes*
Recipe Cook Time: *30–45 minutes*

⅓ cup raw wild honey

3 tablespoons melted coconut oil

½ teaspoon pure vanilla extract

3 cups rolled oats

½ cup chopped raw walnuts

½ cup raw pumpkin seeds

½ cup raw unsalted sunflower seeds

¼ cup unsweetened shredded coconut

1 teaspoon ground cinnamon

½ teaspoon ground cardamom

1 Preheat oven to 325°F. Line a 10" × 15" baking sheet with parchment paper.

2 In a medium bowl, mix together honey, coconut oil, and vanilla.

3 In a large bowl, combine oats, walnuts, pumpkin seeds, sunflower seeds, shredded coconut, cinnamon, and cardamom. Add wet ingredients to dry ingredients and mix well.

4 Spread granola mixture in an even layer on prepared baking sheet. Bake about 30–45 minutes until granola turns golden brown. Remove from oven and let cool at least 20 minutes (the granola will continue to crisp as it cools). Store in an airtight container in the refrigerator for up to a week.

Per Serving

Calories: 354 | Fat: 20.3 g | Protein: 8.9 g | Sodium: 2 mg
Fiber: 5.4 g | Carbohydrates: 36.6 g | Sugar: 12.8 g

Raspberry Breakfast Bars

These fruity breakfast bars are perfect to grab when you're in a rush in the morning, and they'll give you all the protein and carbohydrates you need to start your day with energy. These bars have everything: oats, flaxseed, almond flour, hemp seeds, chia seeds, almond butter. They're also low in sugar, as they're mostly sweetened by the fruit, with just a wee bit of coconut sugar added. Make these bars on a Sunday night so you can have them ready for the rest of the week.

Makes 9 bars

Recipe Prep Time: *20 minutes*
Recipe Cook Time: *35 minutes*

2 tablespoons flaxseed meal
6 tablespoons warm water
1½ cups rolled oats
1 cup almond flour
1 teaspoon baking powder
¼ cup hemp seeds
¼ cup chia seeds
2 tablespoons coconut sugar
1 large ripe banana, peeled and mashed
¼ cup raw crunchy almond butter
1 teaspoon pure vanilla extract
¼ cup unsweetened almond milk
1 cup fresh raspberries

1 Preheat oven to 350°F. Line an 8" × 8" baking pan with parchment paper and grease the sides with cooking spray.

2 In a small bowl, combine flaxseed meal and warm water to create a "flax egg." Stir and let sit 15 minutes until flaxseeds are gummy.

3 In a large bowl, mix together oats, almond flour, baking powder, hemp seeds, chia seeds, and coconut sugar.

4 In a medium bowl, mix together banana, almond butter, vanilla, and flaxseed egg. Pour this mixture into the large bowl, and mix well. Mix in almond milk and raspberries. Don't worry if the raspberries get crushed in the process.

5 Pour the batter into the prepared baking pan and smooth the top with a spoon. Bake 30–35 minutes until edges begin to get crisp and top is golden and firm. Let cool 15 minutes, and then cut into squares.

Per 1 bar

Calories: 239 | Fat: 13.5 g | Protein: 6.3 g | Sodium: 59 mg
Fiber: 6.8 g | Carbohydrates: 23.7 g | Sugar: 6.1 g

Cherry Walnut Breakfast Muffins

Instead of making (or buying!) breakfast pastries filled with sugar, make these gluten-free and vegan muffins that are loaded with protein. Not only are they made with protein powder, but they contain almond flour and walnuts, which provide even more of the nutrient. And while these moist muffins are the perfect grab-and-go option in the morning, they also make a good afternoon snack or even a post-dinner dessert. Enjoy!

Makes 12 muffins

Recipe Prep Time: *10 minutes*
Recipe Cook Time: *30 minutes*

1¼ cups almond flour
1 cup Ginger Pea Protein Powder (Chapter 1)
2 teaspoons baking powder
½ teaspoon sea salt
1 cup mashed ripe banana (about 2 medium bananas)
½ cup unsweetened almond milk
¼ cup pure maple syrup
1 teaspoon pure vanilla extract
¼ cup melted coconut oil
⅓ cup chopped raw walnuts
½ cup dried unsweetened dark sweet cherries

1 Preheat oven to 350°F. Lightly grease a 12-cup muffin tin with cooking spray.

2 In a large bowl, combine flour, protein powder, baking powder, and sea salt.

3 In a medium bowl, combine banana, almond milk, maple syrup, vanilla, and melted coconut oil. Mix until smooth.

4 Pour the wet ingredients into the dry ingredients and stir until combined. Fold in the walnuts and the cherries. Fill up each muffin tin almost to the top with the batter. Bake 25–30 minutes until muffin tops turn golden brown. Remove from oven and let cool 10 minutes before removing from tin.

Per 1 muffin

Calories: 244 | Fat: 12.9 g | Protein: 9.7 g | Sodium: 92 mg
Fiber: 3.5 g | Carbohydrates: 18.2 g | Sugar: 8.5 g

PROTEIN POWDER TOO STRONG?

The pea protein powder used in this recipe tends to have a pretty distinct flavor. It doesn't bother everyone, but if you're not a fan, switch to one of the other protein powders in Chapter 1 or use one of your own.

Kale, Sweet Potato, and Tempeh Breakfast Hash

Breakfast hashes make for a filling breakfast, but they're often served with eggs. For a plant-based alternative, you can use tempeh, which not only provides a good source of protein, but also helps make the dish heartier. And, if you're short on time, you can always microwave the sweet potato instead of baking it, which will cut down your cooking time by about 15 minutes.

Serves 3

Recipe Prep Time: *5 minutes*
Recipe Cook Time: *30 minutes*

1 medium unpeeled sweet potato, diced

2 tablespoons extra-virgin olive oil, divided

2 medium cloves garlic, peeled and finely chopped

½ medium yellow onion, peeled and chopped

3 cups chopped fresh kale

½ cup crumbled organic tempeh

2 tablespoons apple cider vinegar

½ teaspoon paprika

½ teaspoon cayenne pepper

2 tablespoons nutritional yeast

¼ teaspoon black pepper

1 Preheat oven to 425°F. Line a 10" × 15" baking sheet with aluminum foil.

2 Add potatoes and 1 tablespoon oil to a small bowl; toss until evenly coated. Spread potatoes on the prepared baking sheet and bake 20 minutes until potatoes are soft but crispy on the outside.

3 Heat remaining 1 tablespoon oil in a large skillet over medium-low heat. Add garlic and cook 1 minute, stirring so garlic doesn't burn. Add onions and sauté 3 minutes. Add kale and sauté 2 minutes or until it begins to wilt. Add tempeh and cook 1 more minute.

4 Add sweet potatoes to skillet along with vinegar, paprika, cayenne pepper, and yeast. Cook about 1–2 minutes, stirring constantly until well mixed and heated through. Top with black pepper and serve warm.

Per Serving

Calories: 180 | Fat: 9.4 g | Protein: 8.3 g | Sodium: 37 mg
Fiber: 3.0 g | Carbohydrates: 16.3 g | Sugar: 3.0 g

Breakfast Tacos

Breakfast tacos are a fun and unique breakfast, whether you're serving them for brunch or just making them for yourself on a regular morning. Instead of eggs, these tacos are made with a tofu scramble and filled with black beans and spinach for an extra dose of plant-based protein.

Makes 4 tacos

Recipe Prep Time: *10 minutes*
Recipe Cook Time: *8 minutes*

4 (6") corn tortillas
1½ tablespoons extra-virgin olive oil, divided
2 medium cloves garlic, peeled and minced
4 cups fresh spinach leaves
8 ounces extra-firm organic tofu
½ teaspoon ground cumin
1 teaspoon chili powder
¼ teaspoon salt
1½ cups cooked or canned black beans, rinsed and drained
8 cherry tomatoes, halved
1 large avocado, peeled and sliced
Juice of 1 lime

1 Place tortillas on serving plates. In a large pan, heat 1 tablespoon olive oil on medium-low. Add garlic and cook 1 minute. Add spinach and cook 2–3 minutes until wilted. Spoon the spinach on top of the tortillas, dividing it evenly among them.

2 Drain tofu and pat dry with a paper towel. Add to a small bowl and mash with a fork.

3 In the same pan that you used for the spinach, heat remaining ½ tablespoon oil on medium-low. Add tofu, cumin, chili powder, and salt. Mix with a spatula, and cook 1–2 minutes until tofu is evenly coated and warm. Add the tofu to the tortillas on top of the spinach, dividing it evenly among them.

4 Add black beans to the same pan and cook 1–2 minutes until warm. Add the beans to the tacos, dividing them evenly.

5 Top tacos with equal amounts tomatoes, avocado, and lime juice, and serve immediately.

Per 1 taco

Calories: 225 | Fat: 11.8 g | Protein: 10.0 g | Sodium: 215 mg
Fiber: 6.1 g | Carbohydrates: 22.1 g | Sugar: 1.8 g

Pumpkin Pie Chia Seed Pudding

Chia seeds are great to sprinkle on foods, but you can also use them to make a pudding-like treat. All you have to do is mix chia seeds with a tasty beverage such as almond milk and let it sit in the refrigerator overnight, and the seeds will expand in the liquid. This pudding is inspired by the flavors of fall and pumpkin pie, but as long as you have canned pumpkin, you can make it all year long.

Serves 4

Recipe Prep Time: *8 hours*
Recipe Cook Time: *N/A*

1½ cups unsweetened almond milk

½ cup pumpkin purée

1 teaspoon pure vanilla extract

1 teaspoon pumpkin pie spice

⅓ cup chia seeds

1 teaspoon pure maple syrup

¼ teaspoon ground cinnamon

¼ cup chopped pecans

1 In a blender or food processor, blend together almond milk, pumpkin purée, vanilla, and pumpkin spice on high until creamy, about 10 seconds.

2 Add chia seeds and do quick little pulses to mix seeds into liquid. You don't want to blend up the chia seeds, just evenly disperse them.

3 Place mixture into a pint-sized jar or medium bowl, cover, and place into the refrigerator. Let sit overnight or until the pudding is thick in texture. Top with maple syrup, cinnamon, and pecans before serving.

Per Serving

Calories: 136 | Fat: 9.8 g | Protein: 3.6 g | Sodium: 62 mg
Fiber: 6.0 g | Carbohydrates: 9.3 g | Sugar: 1.9 g

Waffles with Chia Blueberry Sauce

Unlike most waffles that are made with refined white flour and sugar, these waffles are made with whole-wheat flour, almond flour, protein powder, and just a bit of coconut sugar, making this dish a much healthier choice. These waffles can also be frozen and reheated later in a toaster, so you can make a big batch and keep them on hand for busy mornings.

Makes 4 waffles

Recipe Prep Time: *15 minutes*
Recipe Cook Time: *13 minutes*

Chia Blueberry Sauce

1 teaspoon coconut oil
1 cup blueberries
3 tablespoons chia seeds
1 tablespoon pure maple syrup

Waffles

¾ cup whole-wheat flour
½ cup almond flour
¼ cup "From Scratch" Protein Powder (Chapter 1)
1½ teaspoons baking powder
3 tablespoons coconut sugar
¼ teaspoon salt
1½ cups unsweetened almond milk
¼ cup melted coconut oil
1 teaspoon pure vanilla extract

1 **For Chia Blueberry Sauce:** In a small saucepan, heat coconut oil on medium heat. Stir in blueberries, chia seeds, and maple syrup and bring to a boil. Reduce to a simmer and cook 4–5 minutes, stirring frequently so the mixture doesn't burn. Remove from heat and set aside. Cover to keep warm.

2 **For Waffles:** Preheat waffle iron on medium-high. In a large bowl, combine flours, protein powder, baking powder, coconut sugar, and salt.

3 In a medium bowl, combine almond milk, melted coconut oil, and vanilla. Pour the wet mixture into the flour mixture and stir until there are no lumps.

4 Spray the waffle iron with cooking spray. Fill the waffle iron with batter almost completely. Close the lid and cook about 6–8 minutes until waffles are golden brown and crisp. Serve immediately, and evenly divide the blueberry sauce on top of each waffle.

Per 1 waffle

Calories: 451 | Fat: 27.5 g | Protein: 7.6 g | Sodium: 390 mg
Fiber: 8.8 g | Carbohydrates: 43.1 g | Sugar: 16.5 g

LOAD UP YOUR WAFFLES

If you want even more protein, consider topping off your waffles with some almond butter in addition to the Chia Blueberry Sauce. Think of it like a peanut butter and jelly sandwich, waffle style.

CHAPTER 3

SMOOTHIES

Sweet Potato Smoothie

Most smoothies are made with a lot of fruit, and although that makes them taste delicious, it can also make them high in sugar. This smoothie is low in sugar because it doesn't contain any fruit—just sweet potato and a little drizzle of maple syrup. The sweet potato helps start your day with healthy carbohydrates and other antioxidants, and almond butter and chia seeds are added for protein. If you want your smoothie to be a little sweeter, just increase the amount of maple syrup by ½ teaspoon and feed your sweet tooth.

Serves 1

Recipe Prep Time: *10 minutes*
Recipe Cook Time: *5 minutes*

1 medium sweet potato, peeled
2 tablespoons raw creamy almond butter
1 tablespoon chia seeds
1 cup unsweetened almond milk
½ teaspoon pure maple syrup
¼ teaspoon ground cinnamon
5 ice cubes

1 Cook sweet potato by poking holes in it with a fork and microwaving 4–5 minutes or until soft. Let cool for a few minutes.

2 Add sweet potato along with all other ingredients to a blender and blend on high speed until smooth, about 10–20 seconds. Serve immediately.

_____

Per Serving

Calories: 378 | Fat: 21.6 g | Protein: 11.8 g | Sodium: 232 mg
Fiber: 11.7 g | Carbohydrates: 39.1 g | Sugar: 9.4 g

Matcha Smoothie

Green tea is one of the healthiest beverages out there, and you can incorporate it into your smoothies by using matcha tea powder. This traditional Japanese drink is as rich in flavor as it is color, and blending it with the banana and cashews gives it some creaminess. The caffeine in the green tea will keep you alert throughout the day, and thanks to the spinach, cashews, and hemp seeds in this smoothie, you'll also get your fair share of antioxidants and protein.

Serves 1

Recipe Prep Time: *10 minutes*
Recipe Cook Time: *N/A*

- 1 cup unsweetened almond milk
- 1 teaspoon matcha powder
- 1 large banana, peeled and sliced
- 1 cup fresh spinach leaves
- 2 tablespoons raw cashews
- 2 tablespoons hemp seeds

Add all ingredients to a blender and blend on high until smooth, about 10–20 seconds. Serve immediately.

Per Serving

Calories: 382 | Fat: 20.3 g | Protein: 14.1 g | Sodium: 186 mg
Fiber: 5.5 g | Carbohydrates: 40.0 g | Sugar: 17.9 g

Orange Ginger Smoothie

This smoothie is perfect for an immune system boost, thanks to the orange juice, turmeric, and ginger, which all help fight off illness. If you want your smoothie to be more of a slushy, you can add some ice to the blender.

Serves 1

Recipe Prep Time: *5 minutes*
Recipe Cook Time: *N/A*

1 medium banana, peeled and broken into pieces
1" knob gingerroot, peeled
¼ cup Ginger Pea Protein Powder (Chapter 1)
1 cup orange juice
¼ teaspoon turmeric powder

Add all ingredients to a blender and blend on high until smooth, about 10–20 seconds. Serve immediately.

Per Serving

Calories: 430 | Fat: 5.7 g | Protein: 29.5 g | Sodium: 13 mg
Fiber: 7.2 g | Carbohydrates: 59.6 g | Sugar: 35.3 g

Vanilla Peach Smoothie

Nothing says summer quite like the combination of peaches and vanilla, and if you like summer, you'll love this refreshing, sweet smoothie. To make sure this smoothie is as pure as possible, make sure to get canned peaches that have no sugar added and that are canned in their natural juices, not syrup. If they're in season, you can definitely use fresh peaches in this smoothie, as long as they are nice and ripe.

Serves 1

Recipe Prep Time: *5 minutes*
Recipe Cook Time: *N/A*

- 1 medium frozen banana, peeled and sliced
- 3 no-sugar-added canned peach halves (use the peaches canned in their natural juices)
- 3 tablespoons canned peach juice (not syrup)
- ½ teaspoon pure vanilla extract
- 1½ cups unsweetened almond milk
- ¼ cup Ginger Pea Protein Powder (Chapter 1)

Add all ingredients to a blender and blend on high until smooth, about 10–20 seconds. Serve immediately.

Per Serving

Calories: 450 | Fat: 9.2 g | Protein: 30.0 g | Sodium: 257 mg
Fiber: 8.1 g | Carbohydrates: 54.8 g | Sugar: 34.2 g

Green Smoothie Bowl

Eating foods with protein is important, but so is eating your vegetables. Green smoothies are a great way to incorporate all your nutrients without having to make separate dishes. This smoothie is thick and topped with a variety of delicious garnishes, so it's best eaten in a bowl, although it can be made into a regular smoothie as well using non-frozen bananas.

Serves 2

Recipe Prep Time: *5 minutes*
Recipe Cook Time: *N/A*

2 frozen medium bananas, peeled and sliced

1 cup fresh spinach leaves

¼ cup Ginger Pea Protein Powder (Chapter 1)

1 cup unsweetened almond milk

4 strawberries, thinly sliced with tops removed

5 blackberries

2 tablespoons chia seeds

1 tablespoon unsweetened shredded coconut

1   Add bananas, spinach, protein powder, and almond milk to a blender and blend on high speed until smooth, about 10–20 seconds.

2   Pour smoothie into a large bowl and top with strawberries, blackberries, chia seeds, and unsweetened coconut. Serve immediately.

Per Serving

Calories: 308 | Fat: 9.0 g | Protein: 17.7 g | Sodium: 99 mg
Fiber: 10.3 g | Carbohydrates: 38.9 g | Sugar: 16.7 g

HOW TO MAKE THE PERFECT SMOOTHIE BOWL

To make a smoothie bowl that stays firm enough to put toppings on, you want to make sure the frozen banana is as cold as possible when you blend it. It's best not to take the banana out of the freezer until you're ready to put it into the blender.

Salted Caramel Smoothie

Ditch that Frappuccino and opt for a homemade Salted Caramel Smoothie instead. This drink doesn't contain any refined sugar, and it gets its decadent caramel taste from the rich Medjool dates. If you want the drink to be even richer and creamier, you can use 1 cup canned coconut milk instead of almond milk.

Serves 1

Recipe Prep Time: *5 minutes*
Recipe Cook Time: *N/A*

1 frozen banana, peeled and sliced

3 Medjool dates

1 cup unsweetened almond milk

⅛ teaspoon salt

¼ cup "From Scratch" Protein Powder (Chapter 1)

Add all ingredients to a blender and blend on high speed until smooth, about 10–20 seconds. Serve immediately.

Per Serving

Calories: 616 | Fat: 23.3 g | Protein: 16.2 g | Sodium: 453 mg Fiber: 17.1 g | Carbohydrates: 93.1 g | Sugar: 62.3 g

BENEFITS OF USING DATES OVER CANE SUGAR

Although it tastes good, cane sugar has absolutely no nutritional value. Dates, on the other hand, contain dietary fiber, antioxidants, and a number of vitamins and minerals.

Breakfast Energy Smoothie

You won't feel guilty about skipping breakfast when drinking this smoothie, as it contains all the energizing nutrients you'll need in the morning. Not only is it loaded with protein, but it also contains complex carbohydrates, healthy fats, and other important vitamins and minerals that will keep you full, alert, and ready to take on the day. Dates are added to help give the smoothie a sweeter taste, but if you don't have dates on hand, you can use a banana.

Serves 1

Recipe Prep Time: *5 minutes*
Recipe Cook Time: *N/A*

½ cup rolled oats
¼ large avocado, peeled
    and pitted
1 tablespoon unsalted
    almond butter
1 tablespoon unsweetened
    cocoa powder
1 tablespoon chia seeds
2 cups unsweetened almond
    milk
3 Medjool dates

Add all ingredients to a blender and blend on high speed until smooth, about 10–20 seconds. Serve immediately.

Per Serving

Calories: 663 | Fat: 27.7 g | Protein: 15.5 g | Sodium: 327 mg
Fiber: 19.8 g | Carbohydrates: 96.3 g | Sugar: 49.8 g

Chocolate Mint Smoothie

This smoothie is inspired by chocolate chip mint ice cream—but it aims to be a little bit healthier. Avocado is added for creaminess along with the almond milk, and spinach is used for additional nutrients and some green color. Fresh mint is used as well as some dark chocolate, and a spoonful of maple syrup is added to give this smoothie some sweetness. And if you want your smoothie even sweeter, just add a banana or extra maple syrup, about ½ tablespoon.

Serves 1

Recipe Prep Time: *5 minutes*
Recipe Cook Time: *N/A*

- ¼ small avocado, peeled and pitted
- 1 cup fresh spinach leaves
- 1 cup unsweetened almond milk
- ¼ teaspoon pure vanilla extract
- 1 tablespoon mint leaves, plus 3 extra for garnish
- ¼ cup "From Scratch" Protein Powder (Chapter 1)
- 1½ tablespoons chopped dark chocolate, plus ¼ teaspoon for garnish
- 1 tablespoon pure maple syrup

In a blender or food processor, blend avocado, spinach, almond milk, vanilla extract, 1 tablespoon mint leaves, protein powder, and 1½ tablespoons dark chocolate together on high speed until smooth, about 10–20 seconds. Garnish with remaining mint leaf and ¼ teaspoon dark chocolate and serve immediately.

Per Serving

Calories: 536 | Fat: 34.6 g | Protein: 16.6 g | Sodium: 192 mg
Fiber: 14.2 g | Carbohydrates: 38.2 g | Sugar: 17.0 g

Chocolate Smoothie

With this delicious Chocolate Smoothie, indulging in your chocolate obsession doesn't have to be unhealthy. This simple recipe is made with plenty of nutritious ingredients, including banana, cocoa powder, spinach, almond milk, and brown rice protein powder, which are all blended together with Medjool dates for some natural sweetness. There are no unhealthy chocolate syrups in this cocoa-filled smoothie, so drink your fill!

Serves 1

Recipe Prep Time: *5 minutes*
Recipe Cook Time: *N/A*

- 1 fresh or frozen banana, peeled and sliced
- ¼ cup Chocolate Cinnamon Brown Rice Protein Powder (Chapter 1)
- 1 tablespoon unsweetened cocoa powder
- 1 cup fresh spinach leaves
- 1 cup almond milk
- 2 Medjool dates
- 1 cup ice cubes

Add all ingredients to a blender and blend on high speed until smooth, about 10–20 seconds. Serve immediately.

Per Serving

Calories: 452 | Fat: 14.2 g | Protein: 12.5 g | Sodium: 192 mg Fiber: 12.3 g | Carbohydrates: 81.7 g | Sugar: 54.4 g

Immune Booster Smoothie

On those days where you are feeling run-down or on the brink of a cold, it's time to make this immune-boosting smoothie. It's filled with vitamin C from the orange juice and lemon as well as powerful antioxidants from the strawberries. The turmeric powder helps fight off inflammation, while the gingerroot can help alleviate any unwanted stomach problems. You also get all the natural nutrients from the various seeds that make up the "From Scratch" Protein Powder. So sip on this Immune Booster Smoothie, and you'll start to feel better in no time!

Serves 1

Recipe Prep Time: *5 minutes*
Recipe Cook Time: *N/A*

1 cup orange juice
½ cup sliced frozen strawberries
½ teaspoon turmeric powder
1" knob gingerroot, peeled
¼ cup "From Scratch" Protein Powder (Chapter 1)
Juice of 1 small lemon

Add all ingredients to a blender and blend on high speed until smooth, about 10–20 seconds. Serve immediately.

Per Serving

Calories: 427 | Fat: 20.8 g | Protein: 14.9 g | Sodium: 5 mg
Fiber: 11.7 g | Carbohydrates: 47.2 g | Sugar: 25.0 g

NEED EVEN MORE OF A BOOST?

There are a number of other immune-boosting ingredients that you can add to your smoothie if you're so inclined. Give spinach, almonds, papaya, kiwi, sunflower seeds, and yogurt a try, and reap the benefits.

Peanut Butter Chocolate Smoothie

There's nothing quite like the combination of peanut butter and chocolate—and while this smoothie tastes like dessert, it's actually loaded with protein-packed, healthy ingredients such as peanut butter and chia seeds. If you would like, you can also top off your smoothie with some cacao nibs or dark chocolate pieces and a drizzle of peanut butter for an extra special drink.

Serves 1

Recipe Prep Time: *5 minutes*
Recipe Cook Time: *N/A*

- 1 frozen banana, peeled and sliced
- 2 tablespoons unsalted creamy raw peanut butter
- 1 tablespoon unsweetened cocoa powder
- ¼ teaspoon pure vanilla extract
- 1 cup unsweetened almond milk
- 1 tablespoon chia seeds

Add all ingredients to a blender and blend on high speed until smooth, about 10–20 seconds. Serve immediately.

Per Serving

Calories: 388 | Fat: 22.6 g | Protein: 13.1 g | Sodium: 163 mg
Fiber: 11.5 g | Carbohydrates: 41.4 g | Sugar: 16.7 g

Strawberry Banana Smoothie

This smoothie Is simple, which makes it perfect for those days when you're in a total rush and don't have time to dig through the cabinet for all the nuts and seeds. As long as you have some protein powder ready, you just need some fruit, almond milk, and some chia seeds to give yourself that much-needed protein boost.

Serves 1

Recipe Prep Time: *5 minutes*
Recipe Cook Time: *N/A*

- 1 cup sliced frozen strawberries
- 1 frozen banana, peeled and sliced
- ¼ cup Ginger Pea Protein Powder (Chapter 1)
- 1 cup unsweetened almond milk
- ¼ cup orange juice
- 1 tablespoon chia seeds

Add all ingredients to a blender and blend on high speed until smooth, about 10–20 seconds. Serve immediately.

Per Serving

Calories: 473 | Fat: 11.2 g | Protein: 31.5 g | Sodium: 174 mg
Fiber: 13.1 g | Carbohydrates: 57.2 g | Sugar: 26.4 g

Antioxidant Blueberry Smoothie

This smoothie may not have a lot of ingredients, but it packs a punch when it comes to both flavor and nutrients. The fruit used here gives you a dose of fiber while the blueberries and the chocolate and cinnamon used in the protein powder help you load up on all your antioxidants. If you're using your own protein powder, you can add 1 teaspoon cocoa powder as well as ¼ teaspoon ground cinnamon to make up for the flavor included in the brown rice protein powder. These two ingredients not only maximize the smoothie's health benefits, but they add a special taste to the drink as well.

Serves 1

Recipe Prep Time: *5 minutes*
Recipe Cook Time: *N/A*

½ cup frozen blueberries
½ frozen banana, peeled and sliced
1 cup unsweetened almond milk
¼ cup Chocolate Cinnamon Brown Rice Protein Powder (Chapter 1)

Add all ingredients to a blender and blend on high speed until smooth, about 10–20 seconds. Serve immediately.

Per Serving

Calories: 258 | Fat: 13.6 g | Protein: 9.4 g | Sodium: 167 mg
Fiber: 7.0 g | Carbohydrates: 29.4 g | Sugar: 14.6 g

WHY DO WE NEED ANTIOXIDANTS?

You've probably heard the word antioxidant, but you might not be quite sure what it means. Antioxidants are vitamins, minerals, and flavonoids that help protect the body from damage caused by free radicals, unstable molecules that damage cells and contribute to aging and disease. Free radicals are formed through natural processes in your body, but they can also be a result of your diet, stress, the environment, etc. Eating antioxidant-rich foods can help fight off disease and slow aging.

Berry Smoothie Bowl

You usually have to add special ingredients to your typical smoothie to make sure it is loaded with protein, but the nice thing about a smoothie bowl is you can put all your favorite foods on top, which helps make it feel like a more complete meal. This berry-filled smoothie bowl does contain protein powder, but it's topped with other protein-rich ingredients like almonds, pumpkin seeds, chia seeds, and oats for even more health benefits.

Serves 2

Recipe Prep Time: *10 minutes*
Recipe Cook Time: *N/A*

2 frozen bananas, peeled and sliced

½ cup sliced frozen strawberries, plus 1 extra strawberry for garnish

½ cup frozen raspberries, plus 2 tablespoons extra for garnish

¼ cup Chocolate Cinnamon Brown Rice Protein Powder (Chapter 1)

2 cups unsweetened almond milk

2 tablespoons sliced almonds

2 tablespoons raw unsalted pumpkin seeds

1 tablespoon chia seeds

¼ cup rolled oats

1 Add bananas, ½ cup strawberries, ½ cup raspberries, protein powder, and almond milk to a blender and blend on high speed until smooth, about 10–20 seconds. Pour into a serving bowl.

2 Top with almonds, pumpkin seeds, chia seeds, oats, and remaining strawberry and 2 tablespoons raspberries. Serve immediately.

Per Serving

Calories: 382 | Fat: 16.9 g | Protein: 12.5 g | Sodium: 166 mg
Fiber: 12.5 g | Carbohydrates: 50.7 g | Sugar: 19.7 g

Mocha Smoothie

Coffee lovers, this smoothie is for you. This Mocha Smoothie is dairy-free, and it gets its protein from the oats and almond butter, which makes this drink a great option for the morning or as an afternoon pick-me-up. Cold brew coffee works best—because it's already cold—but regular coffee works as well. Just make sure to let it cool before you blend it in with everything.

Serves 1

Recipe Prep Time: *5 minutes*
Recipe Cook Time: *N/A*

- 1 frozen banana, peeled and sliced
- ½ cup cold brew coffee
- ½ cup unsweetened almond milk
- 1 tablespoon unsweetened cocoa powder
- ½ cup rolled oats
- 2 tablespoons unsalted almond butter

Add all ingredients to a blender and blend on high speed until smooth, about 10–20 seconds. Serve immediately.

Per Serving

Calories: 479 | Fat: 21.3 g | Protein: 14.7 g | Sodium: 86 mg
Fiber: 12.4 g | Carbohydrates: 63.1 g | Sugar: 16.9 g

Almond Coconut Smoothie

This Almond Coconut Smoothie is perfect for those days when you wish you were sitting under a palm tree sipping out of a coconut. Both coconut milk and shredded coconut are used to give this smoothie a rich coconut flavor, but if you want to cut down on fat, you can use coconut water instead of coconut milk. If you prefer the drink a little sweeter, just add another Medjool date.

Serves 1

Recipe Prep Time: *5 minutes*
Recipe Cook Time: *N/A*

¼ cup canned coconut milk
¼ cup unsweetened almond milk
2 tablespoons raw almond butter
1 tablespoon hemp seeds
1 tablespoon unsweetened shredded coconut
1 Medjool date
½ cup ice

Add all ingredients to a blender and blend on high speed until smooth, about 10–20 seconds. Serve immediately.

Per Serving

Calories: 455 | Fat: 35.8 g | Protein: 12.8 g | Sodium: 48 mg
Fiber: 6.6 g | Carbohydrates: 27.6 g | Sugar: 18.3 g

Tropical Smoothie

Cravings for smoothies usually kick in on warm summer days, and this tropical blend of mango, banana, pineapple, and coconut milk will have you feeling like you're sitting beachside. This island-inspired drink is naturally sweet, refreshing, and extra fruity, and it can be enjoyed even in the winter—if the urge to indulge strikes.

Serves 1

Recipe Prep Time: *5 minutes*
Recipe Cook Time: *N/A*

½ cup cubed frozen mango

1 frozen banana, peeled and sliced

1 cup pineapple juice

½ cup canned coconut milk

¼ cup Ginger Pea Protein Powder (Chapter 1)

1 lemon slice

Add all ingredients to a blender and blend on high speed until smooth, about 10–20 seconds. Garnish with lemon slice. Serve immediately.

Per Serving

Calories: 730 | Fat: 28.2 g | Protein: 30.9 g | Sodium: 30 mg
Fiber: 8.3 g | Carbohydrates: 84.3 g | Sugar: 53.4 g

CHAPTER 4

SALADS AND DRESSINGS

Kale Superfood Salad with Vegan Green Goddess Dressing

Loaded salads taste best with great dressings, but most green goddess dressings are made with ingredients such as anchovies, sour cream, and mayonnaise. Luckily, there's a way to make a healthier version using just plant-based ingredients. This dressing is completely vegan, and it uses avocado and soaked cashews to give you the creaminess you're looking for.

Serves 4

Recipe Prep Time: *15 minutes*
Recipe Cook Time: *15 minutes*

Green Goddess Dressing

½ cup raw unsalted cashews, soaked overnight

1 medium ripe avocado, peeled and pitted

½ cup fresh basil leaves

4 small green onions, sliced

2 large cloves garlic, peeled and finely chopped

Juice of 4 small lemons

¼ cup extra-virgin olive oil

Kale Superfood Salad

6 cups chopped fresh kale leaves

2 tablespoons extra-virgin olive oil, divided

¼ teaspoon sea salt

2 small sweet potatoes, cut into ½" cubes

1 cup cooked green lentils

½ cup halved plum tomatoes

¼ cup raw unsalted sunflower seeds

¼ cup hemp seeds

1 **For Green Goddess Dressing:** Add all dressing ingredients to a blender or food processor and blend on high speed until smooth, about 10–20 seconds.

2 **For Kale Superfood Salad:** Add kale to a large bowl. Add 1 tablespoon olive oil and sea salt, and rub the kale leaves between your fingers to break up the fibers and soften them. Set aside.

3 Preheat oven to 425°F. Line a 10" × 15" baking sheet with aluminum foil.

4 Spread out sweet potatoes on the prepared baking sheet. Drizzle with remaining 1 tablespoon olive oil and bake about 15 minutes until softened and just beginning to crisp.

5 Add sweet potatoes, lentils, tomatoes, sunflower seeds, and hemp seeds to the kale bowl. Add dressing and toss together until everything is evenly coated.

Per Serving
Calories: 563 | Fat: 39.7 g | Protein: 16.4 g | Sodium: 194 mg
Fiber: 11.4 g | Carbohydrates: 24.2 g | Sugar: 7.0 g

Wild Rice Salad with Balsamic Vinaigrette

Most people are used to cooking with white rice or brown rice, so making a dish with wild rice can seem intimidating if you don't know what to expect. However, you won't regret making the switch. Not only does wild rice contain more protein, but it is also high in fiber and other heart-healthy nutrients such as omega-3 fatty acids and linolenic acids. The flavor is a little nutty, which makes it a good addition to salads, and this particular dish balances savory and sweet, thanks to the addition of apples and pomegranate seeds. Wild rice takes some time to prepare, so if you know you're going to make this salad, make the wild rice the night before or at the beginning of the week.

Serves 2

Recipe Prep Time: *10 minutes*
Recipe Cook Time: *50 minutes*

Wild Rice Salad

2 cups water
½ cup wild rice
½ cup cooked chickpeas
2 cups chopped fresh kale leaves
½ cup finely chopped Fuji apples
¼ cup pomegranate seeds
½ large avocado, peeled and diced

Balsamic Vinaigrette

2 tablespoons extra-virgin olive oil
3½ tablespoons balsamic vinegar
1 teaspoon Dijon mustard
1 teaspoon raw wild honey
1 teaspoon dried oregano

1 **For Wild Rice Salad:** Bring water to a boil in a medium pot. Add rice, reduce to a simmer, and cover. Cook 45–50 minutes until rice has softened but is still a bit firm. Remove from heat and let cool 15 minutes.

2 Combine wild rice with remaining Wild Rice Salad ingredients in a large bowl.

3 **For Balsamic Vinaigrette:** Whisk together all dressing ingredients in a small bowl until smooth. Drizzle dressing over salad and toss until evenly coated. Serve immediately.

Per Serving

Calories: 448 | Fat: 19.0 g | Protein: 10.6 g | Sodium: 113 mg
Fiber: 9.6 g | Carbohydrates: 59.3 g | Sugar: 16.2 g

Italian Chopped Salad with Roasted Red Pepper Vinaigrette

This salad is loaded with Italian-inspired goodies like artichoke hearts, pepperoncini, and chickpeas, but the Roasted Red Pepper Vinaigrette is really the star of the show. This dressing really adds some flavor to the salad, so you may want to double or triple the recipe so you can save some in a jar for other salads later on. Dressing should be stored in the refrigerator and will last about a week.

Serves 2

Recipe Prep Time: *20 minutes*
Recipe Cook Time: *N/A*

Italian Chopped Salad

2 cups chopped romaine

2 cups chopped radicchio

¼ cup peeled and thinly sliced red onion

½ cup chopped cherry tomatoes

½ cup chopped artichoke hearts

¼ cup pepperoncini

1½ cups cooked chickpeas

3 tablespoons hemp seeds

Roasted Red Pepper Vinaigrette

½ cup roasted red peppers

1 tablespoon peeled and chopped shallots

½ teaspoon Dijon mustard

3 tablespoons white vinegar

¼ teaspoon dried oregano

¼ teaspoon dried thyme

1 **For Italian Chopped Salad:** Add all salad ingredients to a large bowl.

2 **For Roasted Red Pepper Vinaigrette:** Blend all dressing ingredients together in a blender or food processor on high speed until smooth, about 10 seconds. Pour dressing over salad ingredients and toss. Serve immediately.

Per Serving

Calories: 311 | Fat: 9.0 g | Protein: 16.9 g | Sodium: 628 mg
Fiber: 14.4 g | Carbohydrates: 41.3 g | Sugar: 8.8 g

Purple Kale and White Bean Salad with Lemon Apple Cider Vinaigrette

If you like to make salads quickly, you don't want to have a ton of ingredients to prepare. Fortunately, this salad is simple! It gets its protein from the white beans and chia seeds, which are easy components, since they don't require much preparation. And, if you're looking for something to take with you on the go, this salad is the perfect choice since the kale leaves stay crisp.

Serves 2

Recipe Prep Time: *15 minutes*
Recipe Cook Time: *N/A*

Purple Kale and White Bean Salad

4 cups chopped purple kale leaves

½ cup halved cherry tomatoes

1 medium avocado, peeled and diced

1¼ cup cooked or canned cannellini beans, rinsed and drained

2½ tablespoons chia seeds

¼ teaspoon black pepper

Lemon Apple Cider Vinaigrette

2 tablespoons extra-virgin olive oil

2 tablespoons apple cider vinegar

¼ cup lemon juice

1 **For Purple Kale and White Bean Salad:** Add kale to a large bowl along with tomatoes, avocado, and white beans. Top with chia seeds and pepper.

2 **For Lemon Apple Cider Vinaigrette:** Combine all dressing ingredients in a small bowl. Whisk lightly with a fork.

3 **To finish:** Pour dressing over salad and toss until evenly coated. Serve immediately.

Per Serving

Calories: 483 | Fat: 27.1 g | Protein: 15.3 g | Sodium: 23 mg Fiber: 22.3 g | Carbohydrates: 46.7 g | Sugar: 2.7 g

CAN'T FIND PURPLE KALE?

If you can't find purple kale, don't worry about it. Any variety of kale works well here, so just work with what you've got. It can be fun to switch up your greens, but if a certain type is not available to you, substitutes are always an option.

Springtime Salad

Springtime is filled with bright colors, fresh produce, and an overall feeling of lightness. This Springtime Salad gives you all this and more. It's loaded with produce, including English peas, asparagus, potatoes, and radishes, and it's tossed in a light and refreshing dressing made from just whole-grain mustard, lemon, and apple cider vinegar. If you want to turn this salad into a main dish with extra protein, try adding some lentils.

Serves 4

Recipe Prep Time: *15 minutes*
Recipe Cook Time: *10 minutes*

Salad

1 pound tiny new potatoes (unpeeled)
¾ cup English peas
1 cup shaved asparagus
½ cup thinly sliced radishes
2 medium green onions, finely chopped
2 tablespoons sliced almonds
1 tablespoon lightly chopped fresh dill

Dressing

½ tablespoon whole-grain mustard
2 tablespoons lemon juice
1 tablespoon apple cider vinegar

1. **For Salad:** Add potatoes to a large pot and cover with water. Bring to a boil over medium-high heat and cook 10 minutes or until potatoes are easily pierced with a fork.

2. Meanwhile, bring about ¼ cup water to a boil in a small saucepan; add peas and boil 2 minutes. Drain peas and add to a large salad bowl.

3. Cut the potatoes in half and add to the salad bowl along with asparagus, radishes, green onions, almonds, and dill.

4. **For Dressing:** Whisk together all dressing ingredients in a small bowl until well combined. Add to salad bowl and toss.

Per Serving

Calories: 141 | Fat: 1.6 g | Protein: 5.5 g | Sodium: 24 mg
Fiber: 5.5 g | Carbohydrates: 27.8 g | Sugar: 3.8 g

Kale and Quinoa Tabbouleh with Sliced Almonds and Currants

Tabbouleh is a Middle Eastern dish traditionally made with bulgur. This version is made with quinoa instead, which has more protein than the cracked wheat. Chickpeas are added for extra protein and fiber along with sliced almonds and currants, which give this tabbouleh a little crunchy, sweet twist.

Serves 2

Recipe Prep Time: *10 minutes*
Recipe Cook Time: *15 minutes*

½ cup quinoa

1 cup water

2 cups chopped fresh kale leaves

1 cup cooked chickpeas

¼ cup chopped fresh Italian flat-leaf parsley

¼ cup chopped fresh mint

½ cup chopped cherry tomatoes

3 tablespoons sliced almonds

1 tablespoon dried currants

2 tablespoons extra-virgin olive oil

Juice of 2 small lemons

¼ teaspoon salt

½ teaspoon black pepper

1 Add quinoa and water to a medium saucepan and bring to a boil over medium-high heat. Reduce to a simmer, cover, and cook until all the water is absorbed, about 10–15 minutes. Transfer to a large bowl and let cool 5–10 minutes, until cool to the touch.

2 Add kale, chickpeas, parsley, mint, cherry tomatoes, sliced almonds, and currants to the bowl with the quinoa.

3 Drizzle olive oil and lemon juice over salad, and toss to coat. Season with salt and pepper. Serve immediately or chill.

Per Serving

Calories: 467 | Fat: 21.1 g | Protein: 14.9 g | Sodium: 465 mg
Fiber: 10.9 g | Carbohydrates: 56.1 g | Sugar: 8.6 g

Arugula Salad with Garlic-Roasted Potatoes and Lentils

Potatoes get a bad rap, but they are actually quite healthy—when they're not fried, of course. When added to a salad, potatoes not only add a little bit of protein, but they can help you feel full as well. The garlic-roasted spuds used in this recipe go well with lentils, and the soft, mild texture of the two make a good contrast to the peppery taste of the arugula.

Serves 2

Recipe Prep Time: *15 minutes*
Recipe Cook Time: *30 minutes*

Garlic-Roasted Potatoes

1 medium russet potato, diced
1 tablespoon extra-virgin olive oil
½ teaspoon paprika
½ teaspoon garlic powder
¼ teaspoon black pepper

Arugula Salad

4 cups fresh arugula
1 cup cooked green lentils
½ cup halved cherry tomatoes
½ large avocado, peeled and diced
1 tablespoon extra-virgin olive oil
2 tablespoons white wine vinegar
Juice of 2 small lemons
¼ cup assorted microgreens

1 **For Garlic-Roasted Potatoes:** Preheat oven to 425°F. Line a 10" × 15" baking sheet with aluminum foil. In a medium bowl, toss together potatoes, olive oil, paprika, garlic powder, and pepper. Place on the prepared baking sheet and bake 25–30 minutes or until potatoes are soft and crispy on the edges.

2 **For Arugula Salad:** Combine arugula, lentils, cherry tomatoes, and avocado in a large bowl. When potatoes are finished, add them to the bowl as well. Add olive oil, vinegar, and lemon juice, and toss. Top with assorted microgreens. Serve immediately.

Per Serving

Calories: 378 | Fat: 16.8 g | Protein: 13.5 g | Sodium: 21 mg
Fiber: 13.2 g | Carbohydrates: 45.6 g | Sugar: 5.6 g

Vegan Caesar Salad with Barbecue Tempeh

Caesar salad on its own doesn't contain much protein, which is why chicken is commonly added to the dish. However, this vegan dish ditches the chicken and uses tempeh instead. Tempeh is hearty, cheap, and easy to prepare, and in this recipe, it's made with some barbecue sauce, so you won't miss those meaty flavors!

Serves 4

Recipe Prep Time: *15 minutes*
Recipe Cook Time: *4 minutes*

Caesar Dressing

½ cup raw cashews, soaked
  in water overnight
2 tablespoons Dijon mustard
2 large cloves garlic
Juice of 3 small lemons
2 tablespoons extra-virgin
  olive oil
¼ teaspoon black pepper

Salad

2 heads romaine, chopped
  (about 3 cups chopped)
2 cups chopped fresh kale

Barbecue Tempeh

8 ounces organic tempeh
1 teaspoon extra-virgin olive oil
½ cup barbecue sauce

To Finish

2 tablespoons nutritional yeast

1 **For Caesar Dressing:** Add all dressing ingredients to a food processor or blender and blend on high speed until smooth, about 10–20 seconds.

2 **For Salad:** Add romaine and kale to a large bowl. Add dressing and toss greens until evenly coated.

3 **For Barbecue Tempeh:** In a medium bowl, crumble tempeh with your fingers. Heat 1 teaspoon olive oil in a large sauté pan on medium heat. Add tempeh and barbecue sauce. Cook 3–4 minutes, mixing until evenly coated and heated through.

4 **To finish:** Top salad with barbecue tempeh and nutritional yeast, and serve immediately.

Per Serving

Calories: 370 | Fat: 21.3 g | Protein: 16.2 g | Sodium: 428 mg
Fiber: 2.5 g | Carbohydrates: 30.2 g | Sugar: 14.2 g

CHOOSE THE RIGHT BARBECUE SAUCE

Make sure your barbecue sauce doesn't have very much added sugar or other sugar substitutes like high-fructose corn syrup. It should be made with ingredients you recognize and no funky chemicals or additives. Annie's Naturals carries a good low-sugar option.

Refreshing Mexican Salad

This Mexican-inspired salad is intended to be light and refreshing, almost like you're dining on the beach. It gets its protein from the black beans, corn, and hemp seeds, but it has a tropical twist thanks to the addition of mango and Balsamic Lime Dressing. The frisée adds to that lightness, but this salad would also be tasty with massaged kale instead.

Serves 3

Recipe Prep Time: *15 minutes*
Recipe Cook Time: *5 minutes*

Mexican Salad

½ teaspoon extra-virgin olive oil

1 cup yellow corn kernels

½ bunch frisée, trimmed and cut into 2" pieces

1½ cups canned black beans (rinsed and drained)

¾ cup diced mango

¾ cup chopped cherry tomatoes

Balsamic Lime Dressing

1½ tablespoons extra-virgin olive oil

¼ cup balsamic vinegar

Juice of 2 limes

¼ teaspoon ground cumin

To Finish

½ large avocado, peeled and diced

¼ cup hemp seeds

1. **For Mexican Salad:** In a medium sauté pan, heat oil on medium. Add corn and cook 4–5 minutes or until it begins to soften.

2. Add corn to a large bowl along with remaining salad ingredients.

3. **For Balsamic Lime Dressing:** Whisk together all dressing ingredients in a small bowl until combined.

4. **To finish:** Pour dressing over salad and toss until evenly coated. Top with avocado and hemp seeds.

Per Serving

Calories: 382 | Fat: 17.2 g | Protein: 17.2 g | Sodium: 190 mg
Fiber: 14.9 g | Carbohydrates: 41.8 g | Sugar: 11.5 g

Cucumber and Edamame Salad

This Asian-inspired salad can be served as an entrée for 2 people or a side for 4. It pairs well with noodles and stir-fries, since the Lemon Miso Dressing is light and refreshing. The edamame and cucumber add some crunch to this dish, while the avocado and dressing give the salad some creaminess.

Serves 2

Recipe Prep Time: *15 minutes*
Recipe Cook Time: *N/A*

Salad

2 cups chopped cucumber
1 cup cooked shelled edamame
½ medium avocado, peeled and diced
1 small green onion, finely chopped
2 teaspoons sesame seeds

Lemon Miso Dressing

1 teaspoon red miso paste
Juice of 2 small lemons
1 tablespoon sesame oil
½ teaspoon raw wild honey

1 **For Salad:** Combine salad ingredients in a large bowl.

2 **For Lemon Miso Dressing:** Whisk together all dressing ingredients in a small bowl until smooth.

3 **To finish:** Pour the salad dressing into the large bowl and toss until everything is evenly coated.

Per Serving

Calories: 262 | Fat: 16.0 g | Protein: 11.0 g | Sodium: 133 mg
Fiber: 8.0 g | Carbohydrates: 18.8 g | Sugar: 6.1 g

Barley and Lentil Mushroom Salad

In this salad, the already delicious combo of barley and mushrooms gets a fresh new spin with the addition of chopped romaine, lentils, red onion, goat cheese, and a simple balsamic dressing. It's full of light flavors, but thanks to the protein from the barley and lentils, this dish is hearty and filling enough to eat as a meal, whether it's for lunch or dinner.

Serves 2

Recipe Prep Time: *15 minutes*
Recipe Cook Time: *40 minutes*

½ cup dried green lentils

2½ cups water, divided

½ cup quick-cook barley

2 tablespoons extra-virgin olive oil, divided

1½ cups chopped button mushrooms

3 cups chopped romaine

¼ cup peeled and finely chopped red onion

2½ tablespoons balsamic vinegar

3 tablespoons goat cheese

¼ teaspoon black pepper

1   Add lentils and 1¼ cups water to a medium pot and bring to a boil. Reduce to a simmer, cover, and cook 35–40 minutes or until water is absorbed and lentils have softened.

2   While lentils are cooking, prepare the barley. Add barley and 1¼ cups water to a medium pot and bring to a boil. Reduce heat, cover, and simmer 15 minutes or until barley is cooked. Barley should be tender. When both barley and lentils are done, let cool 10 minutes.

3   While lentils and barley are cooking, prepare mushrooms. Heat 1 tablespoon olive oil on medium-low. Add mushrooms and cook 4–5 minutes until softened. Let mushrooms cool a few minutes.

4   Combine lentils, barley, mushrooms, romaine, and red onion in a large bowl. Toss with remaining 1 tablespoon olive oil and balsamic vinegar. Top with goat cheese and black pepper, and serve immediately.

Per Serving

Calories: 538 | Fat: 16.4 g | Protein: 21.5 g | Sodium: 68 mg
Fiber: 15.3 g | Carbohydrates: 78.2 g | Sugar: 6.9 g

Creamy Lentil Salad with Roasted Tomatoes and Garlic Yogurt Dressing

If you like your salad soft and creamy, this protein-packed salad is for you! In addition to the Garlic Yogurt Dressing, this salad is filled with softness from the cooked lentils, roasted tomatoes, and ripe avocado. If you're vegan, you can substitute the Greek yogurt with 1 tablespoon Dijon mustard or just dress the salad with olive oil and white wine vinegar.

Serves 2

Recipe Prep Time: *10 minutes*
Recipe Cook Time: *40 minutes*

Creamy Lentil Salad

1½ cups cooked green lentils (about 1 cup uncooked)
2½ cups water
1 teaspoon extra-virgin olive oil
1 cup halved cherry tomatoes

Garlic Yogurt Dressing

¼ cup plain 2% Greek yogurt
1 medium clove garlic, peeled and minced
1 teaspoon extra-virgin olive oil
2 tablespoons white wine vinegar

To Finish

¼ cup peeled and thinly sliced small red onion
½ small avocado, peeled and diced
¼ cup chopped fresh Italian flat-leaf parsley
1 teaspoon finely chopped fresh chives

1. **For Creamy Lentil Salad:** Add lentils and water to a medium saucepan, and bring to a boil over medium-high heat. Reduce heat, cover, and simmer until lentils are tender and most of the liquid is absorbed, about 35–40 minutes.

2. While the lentils are cooking, preheat oven to 425°F. Line a small baking sheet with aluminum foil. Add cherry tomatoes to the prepared baking sheet and drizzle with 1 teaspoon olive oil. Roast 20–25 minutes.

3. **For Garlic Yogurt Dressing:** Whisk together all dressing ingredients in a small bowl until smooth.

4. **To finish:** Add lentils, tomatoes, red onion, avocado, and parsley to a large bowl. Toss with dressing and top with chives. Serve immediately.

Per Serving

Calories: 312 | Fat: 10.2 g | Protein: 18.0 g | Sodium: 23 mg
Fiber: 15.4 g | Carbohydrates: 38.7 g | Sugar: 6.5 g

Shaved Brussels Sprouts Salad

Eating whole Brussels sprouts can be intense if you're not used to the flavor, but eating them shaved makes them a little bit more palatable, especially if you're eating them raw in a salad. You can buy preshaved Brussels sprouts at grocery stores like Trader Joe's, or you can shave them yourself using a mandoline or a food processor. And, while this recipe calls for the larger corona white bean, you can use cannellini beans instead.

Serves 2

Recipe Prep Time: *10 minutes*
Recipe Cook Time: *N/A*

4 cups shaved Brussels sprouts

3 tablespoons crushed walnuts

¼ cup shaved Parmesan cheese

1 cup cooked white corona beans (rinsed and drained)

1½ tablespoons extra-virgin olive oil

¼ cup lemon juice

¼ teaspoon black pepper

¼ teaspoon salt

Add all ingredients to a medium bowl and toss together. Serve immediately or refrigerate.

_____

Per Serving

Calories: 434 | Fat: 20.1 g | Protein: 21.1 g | Sodium: 510 mg Fiber: 13.9 g | Carbohydrates: 47.7 g | Sugar: 5.4 g

LOAD UP ON THOSE BRUSSELS

Brussels sprouts are rich in a number of essential vitamins and nutrients, and consuming them can help lower your cholesterol and reduce your risk of cancer. They may not be everyone's favorite vegetable, but they sure do the body good!

Barley Tofu Salad with Pesto Dressing

Thinking about eating tofu in a salad may make you pause, but all that will change when you drizzle on the flavorful pesto dressing used in this recipe. And the plant proteins found in this dish make the salad one you'll come back to again and again. The barley and tofu provide ample protein, but since the dressing contains almonds, you get a little extra boost from that as well. You also don't have to worry about this grain-based salad being too dry, as the pesto not only helps to dress the dish, but the cherry tomatoes and avocado add a refreshing and moist kick that balances out the texture of the tofu and barley.

Serves 2

Recipe Prep Time: *10 minutes*
Recipe Cook Time: *20 minutes*

Pesto Dressing

2 tablespoons sliced almonds

2 medium cloves garlic, peeled and finely chopped

½ cup fresh basil leaves

Juice of 2 small lemons

2 teaspoons extra-virgin olive oil

2 tablespoons apple cider vinegar

Barley Tofu Salad

½ cup quick-cook barley

1½ cups water

1½ teaspoons extra-virgin olive oil

8 ounces organic extra-firm tofu, diced

½ cup chopped cherry tomatoes

½ medium avocado, peeled and diced

1 **For Pesto Dressing:** Add all dressing ingredients to a blender or food processor and blend on medium until smooth, about 10–20 seconds.

2 **For Barley Tofu Salad:** Add barley and water to a pot, and bring to a boil over medium-high heat. Reduce heat and simmer 15 minutes or until barley is cooked. Barley should be tender.

3 Meanwhile, heat oil in a large sauté pan on medium-low. Drain tofu and pat dry with a paper towel. Add tofu to the pan, and cook 5–6 minutes or until tofu is golden brown.

4 **To finish:** Combine barley, tofu, tomatoes, and avocado in a large bowl. Toss with dressing and serve warm or chilled.

Per Serving

Calories: 448 | Fat: 20.7 g | Protein: 18.9 g | Sodium: 18 mg
Fiber: 12.0 g | Carbohydrates: 50.2 g | Sugar: 3.2 g

Picnic Bean Salad

Bean salads are classic picnic options, not only because they're easy to make and carry out the door, but because they retain their flavor and crispness once you arrive to your destination. This Picnic Bean Salad more than suits the bill! With this salad, you don't have to worry about any soggy lettuce, the fresh flavors are perfect for spring and summer, and you'll get lots of protein thanks to the three types of beans.

Serves 6

Recipe Prep Time: *15 minutes*
Recipe Cook Time: *N/A*

Dressing

¼ cup extra-virgin olive oil

2 tablespoons white wine vinegar

1 teaspoon Dijon mustard

1½ teaspoons raw wild honey

½ teaspoon dried basil

½ teaspoon dried oregano

Salad

1 (15-ounce) can black beans, rinsed and drained

1 (15-ounce) can kidney beans, rinsed and drained

1 (15-ounce) can white cannellini beans, rinsed and drained

1 cup chopped red bell pepper

½ cup finely chopped celery

¼ cup peeled and chopped red onion

1 tablespoon chopped fresh Italian flat-leaf parsley

¼ cup lemon juice

½ teaspoon salt

½ teaspoon black pepper

1 **For Dressing:** Whisk together all dressing ingredients in a small bowl until combined.

2 **For Salad:** Combine beans, red pepper, celery, and onion in a large bowl.

3 Add parsley and dressing to the large bowl along with lemon juice, salt, and pepper. Mix together until everything is evenly coated with the dressing. Serve immediately, or refrigerate to chill.

Per Serving

Calories: 216 | Fat: 9.1 g | Protein: 9.1 g | Sodium: 393 mg
Fiber: 9.2 g | Carbohydrates: 24.6 g | Sugar: 3.8 g

Mediterranean Lentil Salad with Hummus Dressing

Time and time again, studies find that the Mediterranean diet is the healthiest, and this is because the focus is on eating lots of plant-based meals. This salad takes inspiration from the region, and it's filled with lots of vegetables, lentils, and some feta cheese for extra flavor. The dressing is also made with hummus for extra protein and a little Mediterranean flair. And if you're in a rush, you can cut your prep time in half by using precooked lentils or by cooking the lentils ahead of time.

Serves 2

Recipe Prep Time: *15 minutes*
Recipe Cook Time: *40 minutes*

Lentil Salad

½ cup dried green lentils
1¼ cups water
3 cups fresh spinach leaves
½ cup chopped artichoke hearts
¼ cup peeled and chopped red onion
½ cup chopped cherry tomatoes
½ cup chopped Persian cucumbers
3 tablespoons crumbled feta cheese
¼ teaspoon black pepper

Hummus Dressing

2 tablespoons Hemp Seed Hummus (Chapter 6)
Juice of 2 small lemons
2 tablespoons apple cider vinegar

1 **For Lentil Salad:** Add lentils and water to a medium pot, and bring to a boil. Reduce to a simmer, cover, and cook 35–40 minutes or until water is absorbed and lentils have softened. Let cool 10–15 minutes.

2 While lentils are cooking, add all remaining salad ingredients to a large salad bowl.

3 **For Hummus Dressing:** Add all dressing ingredients to a blender or food processor and blend on high until smooth, about 10–20 seconds.

4 **To finish:** Add lentils to the salad bowl and toss with dressing. Serve immediately.

Per Serving

Calories: 204 | Fat: 7.1 g | Protein: 11.0 g | Sodium: 316 mg
Fiber: 10.5 g | Carbohydrates: 26.3 g | Sugar: 5.4 g

Sunflower Crunch Salad with Citrus Chia Vinaigrette

This veggie-filled, protein-packed, kale-based salad gets its crunch from the carrots, broccoli, and sunflower seeds. The chia seeds in the dressing add some additional protein, and the lemon and orange in the dressing add a little sweetness. If you want to amp up the protein, you can add some chickpeas or lentils to make this dish a more complete meal.

Serves 2

Recipe Prep Time: *20 minutes*
Recipe Cook Time: *N/A*

Sunflower Crunch Salad

3 cups chopped fresh kale leaves

1 teaspoon extra-virgin olive oil

¼ teaspoon sea salt

1 medium head broccoli, stems removed and florets chopped

3 large carrots, peeled and thinly sliced

⅓ cup peeled and finely chopped red onion

½ cup raw unsalted sunflower seeds

Citrus Chia Vinaigrette

1 tablespoon extra-virgin olive oil

1 tablespoon white wine vinegar

1 teaspoon Dijon mustard

2 tablespoons lemon juice

¼ cup fresh-squeezed orange juice

1 teaspoon chia seeds

1 **For Sunflower Crunch Salad:** Add kale to a large salad bowl along with olive oil and salt. Massage kale leaves with your fingertips to soften the fibers. Add broccoli, carrots, red onion, and sunflower seeds.

2 **For Citrus Chia Vinaigrette:** Add all dressing ingredients to a small bowl and mix with a fork until smooth.

3 **To finish:** Add dressing to salad and toss. Serve immediately.

Per Serving

Calories: 407 | Fat: 24.4 g | Protein: 13.9 g | Sodium: 449 mg
Fiber: 12.6 g | Carbohydrates: 38.2 g | Sugar: 13.3 g

CHAPTER 5

SOUPS AND SANDWICHES

Black Bean Tortilla Soup

It can be hard to find a soup that is both light and filling, but this Black Bean Tortilla Soup is the perfect combination of both. Because it's made with a base of just vegetable broth and diced tomatoes, it won't leave you feeling weighed down. However, it will definitely keep you full thanks to the abundance of protein found in the black beans as well as the corn. This soup is mild, but if you want to make it spicier, you can add some cayenne pepper or even some finely chopped jalapeños.

Serves 6

Recipe Prep Time: *10 minutes*
Recipe Cook Time: *35 minutes*

- 1 tablespoon extra-virgin olive oil
- 4 medium cloves garlic, peeled and minced
- ½ yellow onion, peeled and diced
- 2 teaspoons chili powder
- ½ teaspoon ground cumin
- 2 (15-ounce) cans no-salt-added diced tomatoes
- 2 (15-ounce) cans black beans, rinsed and drained
- 1 cup fresh or frozen yellow corn kernels
- 4 cups low-sodium vegetable broth
- Juice of 2 limes, divided
- ½ cup crumbled tortilla chips, divided
- ¼ cup fresh cilantro leaves, divided
- 1 large avocado, peeled and diced, divided

1. Heat oil in a large pot on medium-low. Add garlic, onion, chili powder, and cumin, stirring together until well combined. Cook 4–5 minutes until onions are translucent.

2. Add tomatoes, beans, corn, and broth, and bring to a boil. Reduce to a simmer, cover, and cook 30 minutes.

3. Divide into 6 individual bowls, and garnish each with equal amounts of lime juice, tortilla chips, cilantro, and avocado. Serve immediately.

Per Serving

Calories: 278 | Fat: 6.8 g | Protein: 13.2 g | Sodium: 376 mg
Fiber: 15.8 g | Carbohydrates: 43.2 g | Sugar: 10.2 g

Lemony Split Pea Soup

Split pea soup is a classic dish that happens to be very high in protein. Many versions include pork, but this vegan soup is loaded with carrots, potatoes, and mushrooms instead. This version is also extra flavorful thanks to the addition of lemon, sage, thyme, and paprika. It's a great dish to cook in bulk and then freeze for later on when you're in a pinch, as it can keep frozen for about 6 months or so.

Serves 4

Recipe Prep Time: *15 minutes*
Recipe Cook Time: *1 hour*

- 1 tablespoon extra-virgin olive oil
- ½ medium yellow onion, peeled and chopped
- ¾ cup peeled and chopped carrots
- ½ pound Yukon gold potatoes, chopped (unpeeled)
- 4 medium cloves garlic, peeled and finely chopped
- ½ pound dried green split peas
- 3 cups low-sodium vegetable broth
- 1 cup water
- ½ cup finely chopped button mushrooms
- 1 tablespoon fresh-chopped sage
- ½ teaspoon dried thyme
- ½ teaspoon paprika
- Juice and zest of 2 small lemons
- ¼ teaspoon black pepper

1 In a large pot, heat oil on medium. Add onion, carrots, potatoes, and garlic; sauté 4–5 minutes, stirring occasionally.

2 Add peas, broth, and water, and bring to a boil over medium-high heat. Stir in mushrooms, sage, thyme, paprika, lemon zest, and lemon juice.

3 Reduce to a simmer, cover, and cook 45–55 minutes or until peas begin to "split" and become mushy. Remove from heat, and serve warm.

Per Serving

Calories: 306 | Fat: 4.0 g | Protein: 15.6 g | Sodium: 135 mg
Fiber: 17.7 g | Carbohydrates: 53.9 g | Sugar: 9.0 g

Chickpea Stew

This recipe is inspired by the chickpea stew recipe from one of my favorite restaurants in Los Angeles, Sqirl. This version has a bit more Moroccan influence with the addition of some flavorful spices. It's also a little lower in salt and a tad more spicy, which is perfect if you're looking to add some extra zing to your life. This soup is delicious served with toasted bread and a dollop of Greek yogurt.

Serves 6

Recipe Prep Time: *8 hours*
Recipe Cook Time: *1 hour 20 minutes*

1 cup dried chickpeas
1 teaspoon salt, divided
3 tablespoons extra-virgin olive oil
1 medium yellow onion, peeled and diced
4 large cloves garlic, peeled and minced
½" knob gingerroot, peeled and finely grated
¼ teaspoon ground cinnamon
1 teaspoon chili powder
1 teaspoon ground cumin
¾ teaspoon red pepper flakes
3 (28-ounce) cans no-salt-added whole tomatoes, chopped
3 cups sliced rainbow chard (stems removed)
Juice of 1 small lemon

1 Add chickpeas to a large bowl and cover with water. Soak overnight.

2 Rinse and drain chickpeas; add to a large pot with ½ teaspoon salt and 4 cups fresh water and bring to a boil. Reduce to a simmer, cover, and cook about 50–55 minutes until chickpeas are soft. Add water as needed if the water starts to evaporate and the chickpeas are no longer submerged.

3 Pour the chickpeas, along with the water, into a large bowl; set aside. In the empty pot, heat oil on medium-low. Cook onions 3–4 minutes until translucent, stirring occasionally. Add garlic, ginger, cinnamon, chili powder, cumin, red pepper flakes, and remaining ½ teaspoon salt, and stir together. Cook 1 minute.

4 Add tomatoes to the pot and increase heat to medium-high. Cook 10 minutes, stirring occasionally.

5 Add chickpeas with their liquid. Bring to a boil, reduce to a simmer, and cook 5 minutes. During the last minute, mix in the chard and lemon juice. Serve warm.

Per Serving

Calories: 301 | Fat: 8.3 g | Protein: 10.9 g | Sodium: 448 mg
Fiber: 11.6 g | Carbohydrates: 44.5 g | Sugar: 14.5 g

NO TIME TO SOAK THE CHICKPEAS?

If you decide to make this soup at the last minute and you haven't soaked your chickpeas overnight, don't fear. You can still cook the chickpeas as is; they will just require a longer cook time in the pot, about 30 minutes longer.

Green Lentil Soup

This beautiful green lentil soup gets its color not only from the green lentils, but from the kale, parsley, and green onion as well. The coconut milk gives it extra richness and creaminess, and a squeeze of lemon gives it a citrus kick. If you ever feel like you need a detox, this soup should be your go-to. You'll feel refreshed and revived thanks to the protein in the lentils and the anti-inflammatory properties of the garlic and turmeric.

Serves 6

Recipe Prep Time: *15 minutes*
Recipe Cook Time: *45 minutes*

- 1 tablespoon extra-virgin olive oil
- 1 large yellow onion, peeled and chopped
- 4 cloves garlic, peeled and minced
- 1 cup dried green lentils, rinsed
- 4 cups low-sodium vegetable broth
- 1½ cups canned coconut milk
- ½ teaspoon turmeric powder
- ½ teaspoon ground thyme
- Juice of 1 small lemon
- 7 cups chopped fresh kale leaves
- ½ cup chopped fresh Italian flat-leaf parsley
- 5 small green onions, chopped into 1" pieces

1 Heat oil in a large pot on medium heat. Add yellow onion and garlic, and cook 4–5 minutes until onions are translucent.

2 Add lentils, vegetable broth, coconut milk, turmeric, and thyme; bring to a boil. Reduce to a simmer, cover, and cook 20 minutes.

3 Add lemon juice, kale, parsley, and green onion, and stir well. Cover and cook an additional 20 minutes. Serve warm.

Per Serving

Calories: 276 | Fat: 13.9 g | Protein: 10.3 g | Sodium: 106 mg
Fiber: 5.4 g | Carbohydrates: 29.0 g | Sugar: 3.5 g

Quinoa Chili

You don't need meat in your chili to get your fair share of protein. Instead, you can enjoy this protein-full bowl of quinoa, kidney beans, and black beans that are cooked with garlic, onions, red pepper, jalapeños, and spices for guaranteed flavor. This chili isn't too spicy—it just has a subtle kick—but if you want to up the ante, you can use a whole jalapeño instead of half. This bowl also tastes great topped with some avocado and Greek yogurt.

Serves 6

Recipe Prep Time: *15 minutes*
Recipe Cook Time: *35 minutes*

1 tablespoon extra-virgin olive oil

1 medium yellow onion, peeled and diced

4 medium cloves garlic, peeled and minced

½ small red bell pepper, seeded and chopped, plus ¼ cup extra for garnish

1 (15-ounce) can no-salt-added diced tomatoes

½ small jalapeño, finely chopped, plus ¼ jalapeño thinly sliced for garnish

2 tablespoons chili powder

2 teaspoons paprika

1 teaspoon ground cumin

½ teaspoon ground cinnamon

¼ teaspoon salt

1½ cups low-sodium vegetable broth

1 cup quinoa

1 (15-ounce) can black beans, rinsed and drained

1 (15-ounce) can kidney beans, rinsed and drained

2 small green onions, finely chopped

1 In a large pot, heat oil on medium heat. Add onion, garlic, and the half bell pepper. Cook about 4 minutes, stirring occasionally.

2 Add tomatoes, chopped jalapeño, chili powder, paprika, cumin, cinnamon, salt, and broth. Stir and bring to a boil. Add quinoa, black beans, and kidney beans; reduce to a simmer and cover. Cook 30 minutes, stirring occasionally.

3 Top with green onion and sliced jalapeño and ¼ cup chopped red pepper. Serve warm.

Per Serving

Calories: 283 | Fat: 4.8 g | Protein: 13.4 g | Sodium: 429 mg
Fiber: 13.7 g | Carbohydrates: 48.1 g | Sugar: 4.5 g

White Bean Tomato Soup

Tomato soup is a classic, but it's often filled with cream or other rich ingredients. This recipe uses white beans for protein, which makes the soup heartier. You can eat this soup as a side or as an entrée, and you might want to whip it up when you're craving some veggies, as it's loaded with carrots, tomatoes, and kale.

Serves 4

Recipe Prep Time: *15 minutes*
Recipe Cook Time: *30 minutes*

- 1 tablespoon extra-virgin olive oil
- 1 medium yellow onion, peeled and diced
- 4 medium cloves garlic, peeled and chopped
- 1 large carrot, chopped
- 2 cups crushed tomatoes
- 1 teaspoon dried thyme
- ¼ teaspoon black pepper
- ¼ teaspoon salt
- 3 cups low-sodium vegetable broth
- 2 cups canned cannellini beans (rinsed and drained)
- 3 cups roughly chopped fresh kale
- 2 tablespoons raw sliced almonds

1. In a medium pot, heat olive oil on medium heat. Add onions, garlic, and carrots, and cook 4–5 minutes until onions are translucent and carrots begin to soften.

2. Stir in tomatoes, thyme, pepper, and salt. Bring to a light boil, and then lower heat to medium-low. Simmer lightly 10 minutes, stirring occasionally.

3. Add broth and cannellini beans. Bring to a boil. Add kale and reduce to a simmer. Cover and cook 15 minutes to let the flavors meld.

4. Top with almonds before serving.

Per Serving

Calories: 235 | Fat: 5.3 g | Protein: 11.4 g | Sodium: 487 mg
Fiber: 10.6 g | Carbohydrates: 38.0 g | Sugar: 9.3 g

Wild Rice Mushroom Soup

When you're feeling sick, this wild rice soup with mushrooms and chickpeas is the perfect substitute for chicken noodle soup. This dish gets its protein from the wild rice and chickpeas, as well as fiber from the rice and other vegetables, including celery and carrots. It's also filled with garlic and herbs, which add a strong, hearty flavor to the vegetable broth.

Serves 6

Recipe Prep Time: *10 minutes*
Recipe Cook Time: *1½ hours*

1 cup wild rice

3 cups water

1 tablespoon olive oil

1 large yellow onion, peeled and chopped

4 stalks celery, chopped

2 medium carrots, chopped

8 ounces button mushrooms, chopped

2 small cloves garlic, peeled and finely chopped

1 teaspoon dried oregano

1 teaspoon fresh thyme

2 tablespoons whole-wheat flour

1 bay leaf

1 quart vegetable stock

1 (15-ounce) can chickpeas, rinsed and drained

½ teaspoon salt

¼ teaspoon black pepper

1 Prepare wild rice by bringing water to a boil in a large pot. Add rice, reduce to a simmer, and cover. Cook 45–50 minutes until rice has softened but is still a bit firm.

2 In a separate large pot, heat olive oil on medium heat. Add onions, celery, and carrots, and cook 3–5 minutes until onions are translucent. Add mushrooms and cook 10–15 minutes until mushrooms are very soft.

3 Add garlic, oregano, and thyme to the pan and cook 1 minute. Add flour and stir until it dissolves. Add bay leaf and vegetable stock, and bring to a boil. Reduce to a simmer, cover, and cook 20 minutes. Add cooked wild rice, chickpeas, salt, and pepper, and cook 1–2 minutes until heated through. Serve warm.

Per Serving

Calories: 215 | Fat: 2.8 g | Protein: 9.1 g | Sodium: 688 mg
Fiber: 6.5 g | Carbohydrates: 39.9 g | Sugar: 6.6 g

Smashed Chickpea and Avocado Sandwich

Chickpeas are a great go-to protein, but people get so used to adding them to salads that they forget they can be mashed up to be used as a filling for sandwiches. This is a vegan-friendly sandwich that is flavorful, filling, and takes only 10 minutes to make. Plus, there's no need for mayo, thanks to the natural creaminess of the avocado!

Serves 2

Recipe Prep Time: *10 min*
Recipe Cook Time: *N/A*

1 (15-ounce) can chickpeas, rinsed and drained

1 medium ripe avocado, peeled and pitted

1 tablespoon chopped fresh cilantro

¼ teaspoon salt

¼ teaspoon black pepper

1 teaspoon extra-virgin olive oil

Juice of 2 small lemons

4 thin slices whole-grain bread

½ cup fresh arugula

1 In a medium bowl, combine chickpeas and avocado. Mash together with a fork until blended but still a bit chunky. Mix in cilantro, salt, pepper, olive oil, and lemon juice.

2 Spread chickpea mixture onto 2 slices of bread. Top with arugula and remaining bread slices. Serve immediately or refrigerate. Sandwich will last a few hours.

Per Serving

Calories: 477 | Fat: 15.5 g | Protein: 18.5 g | Sodium: 856 mg Fiber: 16.7 g | Carbohydrates: 64.7 g | Sugar: 8.9 g

White Bean Collard Green Wrap with Lemon Aioli

If you enjoy wraps, collard greens are a great nutrient-filled alternative to using a tortilla made from refined flour. Collard greens are sturdy, so you can load them up with many fillings without having to worry about your wrap falling apart. When choosing your collard greens, be sure to choose the largest leaves possible so you can pack them with this delicious filling that's loaed with white beans for protein and avocado for healthy fats—both of which work to keep you full and satisfied.

Makes 2 wraps

Recipe Prep Time: *15 minutes*
Recipe Cook Time: *1 minute*

Wrap
2 large collard green leaves
½ cup chopped oil-packed sun-dried tomatoes
1 medium avocado, peeled and sliced
1½ cups canned cannellini beans (rinsed and drained)

Lemon Aioli
2 tablespoons Vegenaise
Juice of 1 small lemon
1 teaspoon garlic powder

1 **For Wrap:** Cut out and discard the thick part of the collard green stalks. Bring a small pot of water to a boil and steam the leaves over the boiling water until softened, about 1 minute.

2 Place an even amount of sun-dried tomatoes in the center of each collard green, leaving plenty of space around the edges. Top with avocado and cannellini beans, dividing them equally between the leaves.

3 **For Lemon Aioli:** Whisk together all aioli ingredients in a small bowl until smooth. Drizzle over fillings in the middle of the wrap.

4 **To finish:** Roll up each wrap tortilla-style by folding one side of the leaf over the top of the filling and tucking it underneath. Fold in the sides and continue to roll from top to bottom, keeping the sides snuggly tucked in. Once the wraps are rolled, slice in half crosswise and secure with a toothpick. Serve immediately.

Per 1 wrap

Calories: 444 | Fat: 22.4 g | Protein: 15.1 g | Sodium: 167 mg
Fiber: 15.6 g | Carbohydrates: 46.7 g | Sugar: 1.1 g

Spinach and Pumpkin Seed Pesto Grilled Cheese

Grilled cheese is the ultimate comfort food, but it doesn't have to always be a guilty pleasure. Tofu is added to this version to help cut down on the amount of cheese used as well as to provide that much-needed plant protein. You also get more protein from the spinach and the Pumpkin Seed Pesto. If you are vegan, opt for vegan cheese slices and use olive oil in place of ghee.

Serves 2

Recipe Prep Time: 15 minutes
Recipe Cook Time: 10 minutes

Pumpkin Seed Pesto

⅓ cup raw unsalted pumpkin seeds
2 medium cloves garlic, peeled and chopped
⅓ cup fresh basil leaves
1 tablespoon extra-virgin olive oil
Juice of 1 small lemon
1 teaspoon filtered water

Sandwiches

1 teaspoon extra-virgin olive oil
4 cups fresh spinach leaves
6 ounces extra-firm organic tofu
4 thin slices sprouted-grain bread
2.5 ounces Gruyère cheese, sliced
2 teaspoons ghee, divided

1. **For Pumpkin Seed Pesto:** Add all pesto ingredients to a food processor or blender and blend on medium until smooth, about 10–20 seconds.

2. **For Sandwiches:** Heat olive oil in a large pan on medium-low heat. Add spinach leaves and cook 1–2 minutes until spinach wilts; set aside.

3. Drain liquid from tofu and pat dry with a paper towel. Mash tofu with a fork until softened.

4. Spread Pumpkin Seed Pesto on 2 slices bread. Add cheese slices to the other 2 slices bread along with tofu and wilted spinach and top with pesto-covered bread slices.

5. Heat 1 teaspoon ghee in a large skillet on medium heat. Once the butter is hot, add the sandwiches and press down with a spatula to flatten. Cover and cook 3–4 minutes until golden brown on bottom. Remove the sandwiches with a spatula, add the remaining 1 teaspoon ghee, and cook on the other side until golden brown and the cheese is melted, about 3–4 minutes. Serve immediately.

WHY USE FILTERED WATER?

Although you can use tap water, using filtered water in the pesto is preferred, as it helps the pesto taste better.

Per Serving

Calories: 631 | Fat: 38.5 g | Protein: 35.6 g | Sodium: 458 mg
Fiber: 9.1 g | Carbohydrates: 38.5 g | Sugar: 1.5 g

Hummus Avocado Sandwich with Spinach and Roasted Red Pepper

Veggie sandwiches can be quite tasty and feel like a light option, but they often lack the proper nutrients to keep you full and satisfied. You won't have that problem with this sandwich, since its main ingredient is protein-filled hummus. If you'd like, you can use the Hemp Seed Hummus from Chapter 6, or use a hummus of your own.

Makes 1 sandwich

Recipe Prep Time: *10 minutes*
Recipe Cook Time: *N/A*

2 thin slices multigrain sourdough bread
⅓ cup Hemp Seed Hummus (Chapter 6)
¾ cup fresh spinach leaves
½ cup sliced roasted red peppers
½ medium avocado, peeled and sliced

1 Toast both slices bread until just golden. Spread hummus on 1 slice of bread. Top with spinach and red pepper.

2 On the other piece of bread, add avocado. Combine both sides, and cut in half.

Per 1 sandwich

Calories: 611 | Fat: 34.9 g | Protein: 17.6 g | Sodium: 662 mg
Fiber: 12.1 g | Carbohydrates: 56.5 g | Sugar: 7.5 g

Lentil Pita

Both pita bread and lentils are commonly used in Middle Eastern and Mediterranean cuisine, so it makes sense that they would pair well together. The lentil filling found in this dish can be made extremely quickly, and you can even make extra to enjoy in a salad. One whole pita pocket cut in half will work for 2 servings—just opt for whole-wheat pitas over white pitas, which are not only healthier, but contain more protein as well.

Serves 2

Recipe Prep Time: *10 minutes*
Recipe Cook Time: *N/A*

1½ cups cooked green lentils

½ cup chopped tomatoes

¼ cup peeled and chopped red onion

¼ cup plain 2% Greek yogurt

Juice of 1 small lemon

1 tablespoon extra-virgin olive oil

¼ teaspoon dried oregano

¼ teaspoon salt

¼ teaspoon black pepper

1 (6½") whole-wheat pita pocket

1 Mix together lentils, tomatoes, onion, yogurt, lemon, olive oil, oregano, salt, and pepper in a medium bowl.

2 Cut pita in half and scoop the mixture into each side. Serve immediately.

Per Serving

Calories: 365 | Fat: 8.2 g | Protein: 20.3 g | Sodium: 447 mg
Fiber: 15.5 g | Carbohydrates: 55.4 g | Sugar: 7.3 g

Edamame Wrap

When it comes to using plant-based proteins in a sandwich, edamame might not be the first thing that comes to mind. However, rather than smashing some soy beans between two pieces of bread, you can delicately wrap them up in a tortilla and throw in some quinoa for extra protein. If you want to cut down on carbs, feel free to use a large collard green leaf as a wrap instead, but the brown rice tortilla does add a little extra protein to this unique dish.

Makes 2 wraps

Recipe Prep Time: *10 minutes*
Recipe Cook Time: *N/A*

2 (10") brown rice tortillas
½ cup cooked quinoa
½ cup cooked shelled edamame
1 Persian cucumber, thinly sliced
1 small carrot, peeled and thinly sliced
½ avocado, peeled and sliced
2 tablespoons low-sodium soy sauce
Juice of 1 small lemon

1   Lay tortillas flat. Spoon half the quinoa in the center of each tortilla. Top each with equal amounts of edamame, cucumber, carrots, and avocado.

2   Drizzle soy sauce and lemon juice over the contents of the wraps.

3   To wrap, fold one side of the tortilla over the filling and tuck it under, then fold the sides in. Keeping the sides tucked in, roll the tortilla tightly to close up the wrap.

Per 1 wrap

Calories: 326 | Fat: 9.7 g | Protein: 11.2 g | Sodium: 703 mg
Fiber: 9.4 g | Carbohydrates: 47.9 g | Sugar: 4.8 g

TLT: Tempeh Lettuce Tomato Sandwich

This vegan take on a BLT uses tempeh "bacon," which is what makes it a TLT. Here, the tempeh is seared and crisped to perfection in a maple pepper marinade and then combined with the classic ingredients of lettuce and tomato, with some creamy avocado. The sprouted-grain bread used in this recipe adds even more protein to the sandwich, and it is much more nutritious than white bread.

Makes 3 sandwiches

Recipe Prep Time: *15 minutes*
Recipe Cook Time: *10 minutes*

Tempeh "Bacon"
8 ounces organic tempeh
2 tablespoons extra-virgin olive oil
2 tablespoons pure maple syrup
¼ teaspoon paprika
¼ teaspoon cayenne pepper
¼ teaspoon black pepper

Sandwich
6 slices sprouted-grain bread
1½ tablespoons Vegenaise
1 medium avocado, peeled and sliced
1 medium tomato, thinly sliced
6 butter lettuce leaves

1 **For Tempeh "Bacon":** Cut tempeh into 3 thin strips widthwise, then cut those strips in half lengthwise. Cut them in half once more, this time crosswise. You should have 12 bacon-like strips that are about 1" wide and 3" long.

2 In a medium bowl, combine olive oil, maple syrup, paprika, cayenne pepper, and black pepper. Spread half the mixture onto one side of all the tempeh strips. Heat a large pan on medium heat. Add tempeh (sauce-side down) and cook 5 minutes until golden and beginning to char. Coat the top with the remaining sauce and flip the tempeh; cook another 5 minutes.

3 **For Sandwich:** Toast bread. Spread mayo on 3 slices bread. Add tempeh, and top with avocado, tomato, and lettuce. Top with remaining slices of bread and serve immediately.

Per 1 sandwich

Calories: 550 | Fat: 27.4 g | Protein: 23.5 g | Sodium: 206 mg
Fiber: 9.9 g | Carbohydrates: 52.6 g | Sugar: 9.4 g

Black Bean Burgers with Arugula, Avocado, and Sriracha Mayo

These easy-to-prepare black bean burgers don't require any special kitchen tools, and they can help satisfy those cravings when you want to use plant-based proteins, but also want to take a big bite out of something "meaty." These bean-based burgers mimic a medium-rare burger, as they're slightly softer on the inside and crisp on the outside, but if you want your burger more firm all around, you can add an egg to the mixture to act as a binder.

Makes 4 burgers

Recipe Prep Time: *15 minutes*
Recipe Cook Time: *15 minutes*

Burger Patties

2½ cups canned black beans
    (rinsed and drained)
1 medium yellow onion,
    peeled and grated
¼ cup flaxseed meal
¼ teaspoon garlic powder
¼ teaspoon cayenne pepper
½ teaspoon ground cumin
¼ teaspoon salt
¼ teaspoon black pepper
¼ cup extra-virgin olive oil

Sriracha Mayo

2 tablespoons Vegenaise
1½ teaspoons sriracha

To Finish

4 whole-grain hamburger
    buns
1 medium avocado, peeled
    and sliced
1 cup fresh arugula
1 medium tomato, sliced

1 **For Burger Patties:** In a large bowl, mash black beans with a fork until softened but still firm enough to form into patties. Add grated onion, flaxseed meal, garlic powder, cayenne pepper, cumin, salt, and pepper. Form mixture into 4 equal patties using your hands (keep in mind that the patties will stay the same size when you cook them).

2 In a large pan, heat oil on medium-low. Add patties to the pan and cook 5–7 minutes on each side until dark and crispy.

3 **For Sriracha Mayo:** Mix together Vegenaise and sriracha in a small bowl until smooth.

4 **To finish:** Toast the buns in toaster to desired doneness. Spread the mayo on the bottom of each burger bun and top with a patty. Top each patty with avocado, arugula, and tomato. Serve immediately.

Per 1 burger

Calories: 525 | Fat: 27.3 g | Protein: 16.1 g | Sodium: 627 mg
Fiber: 16.8 g | Carbohydrates: 53.8 g | Sugar: 5.4 g

Tofu Banh Mi

Banh mi sandwiches are the result of both Vietnamese and French influence, with the baguette, jalapeño, and mayonnaise components coming from the French, and the pickled vegetables and herbs like cilantro coming from the Vietnamese. Typical traditional banh mi sandwiches contain Vietnamese cold cuts, but this plant-protein version uses ginger-marinated tofu instead. If you want to add some spice, this banh mi tastes delicious with a drizzle of sriracha on top.

Serves 2

Recipe Prep Time: *1 hour 15 minutes*
Recipe Cook Time: *12 minutes*

Pickled Vegetables

¼ English cucumber, sliced thinly crosswise

1 medium carrot, peeled and cut into thin slices

½ small jalapeño, thinly sliced crosswise

¼ cup white wine vinegar

¼ cup rice vinegar

¼ teaspoon coconut sugar

¼ teaspoon salt

Tofu

2 medium cloves garlic, peeled and minced

1" knob gingerroot, grated

Juice of 2 small lemons

2 tablespoons low-sodium soy sauce

8 ounces extra-firm organic tofu, cut into ½" slices

½ tablespoon sesame oil

To Finish

2 tablespoons Vegenaise

½ baguette, cut in half lengthwise

1 tablespoon chopped fresh cilantro

1 **For Pickled Vegetables:** Combine all ingredients in a large bowl or jar. Stir everything together and make sure vegetables are submerged. Let sit at least 1 hour to pickle or even overnight if a strong taste is desired.

2 **For Tofu:** Combine garlic, ginger, lemon, and soy sauce in a medium bowl. Add sliced tofu and spoon the mixture over the tofu to marinate. Let sit 30 minutes in the refrigerator.

3 Heat sesame oil in a large pan on medium. Add tofu and cook 3–6 minutes on each side until both sides are crispy.

4 **To finish:** Spread Veganaise on one side of the baguette. Add the pickled vegetables, tofu, and cilantro. Top with the other side of the baguette. Cut in half widthwise to make 2 servings and serve immediately.

Per Serving

Calories: 422 | Fat: 17.4 g | Protein: 20.1 g | Sodium: 1,294 mg
Fiber: 3.2 g | Carbohydrates: 45.1 g | Sugar: 7.1 g

Spicy Edamame and Tofu Ramen

Traditional ramen bowls are laden with animal fat, but not this version! This Spicy Edamame and Tofu Ramen is flavored with vegetable broth, mushroom broth, miso, soy sauce, and sriracha with tofu and edamame bringing the protein to the party. Even the noodles here are healthy and protein-filled, since this recipe calls for brown rice ramen noodles instead of the typical ramen noodles. This ramen is on the spicier side, so if you want it milder, cut the amount of sriracha used in half.

Serves 4

Recipe Prep Time: *30 minutes*
Recipe Cook Time: *25 minutes*

½ ounce (7 grams) dried shiitake mushrooms

1 tablespoon sesame oil

4 large cloves garlic, peeled and finely chopped

1 quart low-sodium vegetable broth

3 tablespoons red miso paste

¼ cup low-sodium soy sauce

2 teaspoons sriracha

10 ounces brown rice ramen noodles

3 ounces bok choy

1 cup organic shelled edamame

4 ounces extra-firm organic tofu, diced into small squares

2 small green onions, thinly sliced

1 Add dried mushrooms to a bowl and cover with boiling water. Let sit 20 minutes.

2 In a large pot, heat sesame oil on medium-low. Add garlic and cook 1 minute, stirring occasionally. Add broth, miso paste, soy sauce, sriracha, and soaked mushrooms along with their liquid, and bring to a boil. Reduce to a simmer and cook 15 minutes. While broth is cooking, prepare noodles according to package directions.

3 Add bok choy and edamame to broth and cook an additional 5 minutes.

4 To serve, add noodles to a bowl and cover with broth. Top with tofu squares and green onions and serve immediately.

Per Serving

Calories: 466 | Fat: 12.4 g | Protein: 21.9 g | Sodium: 1,402 mg
Fiber: 9.2 g | Carbohydrates: 65.7 g | Sugar: 6.2 g

CHAPTER 6

SNACKS AND APPETIZERS

Hemp Seed Hummus

Most people enjoy hummus as a snack served with some vegetables or pita chips, and because it's made with chickpeas, it's a great source of protein. This Hemp Seed Hummus, however, gets an even bigger boost of the nutrient thanks to the addition of the hemp seeds, which adds about 14 grams of protein to the dish. Feel free to experiment with different flavors by adding some sun-dried tomatoes, red pepper, or any of your favorite herbs for extra flavor.

Serves 4

Recipe Prep Time: *10 minutes*
Recipe Cook Time: *N/A*

3 tablespoons plus 1 teaspoon hemp seeds, divided

1 (15-ounce) can chickpeas, rinsed and drained

1 tablespoon tahini

2 medium cloves garlic, peeled and minced

1 tablespoon lemon juice

5 tablespoons extra-virgin olive oil, divided

2 tablespoons filtered water

¼ teaspoon salt

½ teaspoon dried parsley

3 fresh basil leaves

1 In a food processor or blender, grind 3 tablespoons hemp seeds on high speed about 10 seconds until a smooth paste forms. Add chickpeas, tahini, garlic, lemon juice, 4 tablespoons olive oil, water, and salt. Blend on high speed until smooth, about 10–20 seconds.

2 Transfer to a bowl and top with remaining olive oil and hemp seeds. Top with parsley, and add basil for garnish. Hummus should be stored in the refrigerator and is good up to 3 days.

Per Serving

Calories: 309 | Fat: 23.2 g | Protein: 8.3 g | Sodium: 284 mg
Fiber: 4.7 g | Carbohydrates: 16.6 g | Sugar: 2.7 g

Mexican Loaded French Fries

This cross between french fries and nachos might sound unhealthy, but these Mexican Loaded French Fries are made with clean ingredients, and the fries are baked, not fried. The potatoes and black beans add protein to the dish, and the mashed lemony avocado tops off the fries with extra flavor. If you're a fan of heat, try adding some jalapeños or hot sauce to make this dish even more amazing.

Serves 3

Recipe Prep Time: *10 minutes*
Recipe Cook Time: *25 minutes*

- 2 russet potatoes, sliced into thin, fry-sized wedges
- 2 tablespoons extra-virgin olive oil
- 1 large ripe avocado, peeled and pitted
- 2 tablespoons lemon juice
- ½ teaspoon garlic powder
- ¼ teaspoon salt
- ¼ teaspoon black pepper
- 1 cup canned black beans (rinsed and drained)
- ¾ cup chopped cherry tomatoes
- 2 small green onions, finely chopped
- 2 tablespoons assorted microgreens

1 Preheat oven to 425°F. Line a 10" × 15" baking sheet with aluminum foil. Spread potatoes evenly onto baking sheet and drizzle with olive oil. Bake 10 minutes and then remove from oven. Turn potatoes and bake another 15 minutes. Potatoes should be crisp on the outside but soft inside.

2 While potatoes are baking, scoop out avocado and place it in a medium bowl. Add lemon juice, garlic powder, salt, and pepper, and mash with a fork.

3 When potatoes are ready, top with black beans, tomatoes, green onion, avocado mash, and microgreens. Serve immediately.

Per Serving

Calories: 415 | Fat: 13.2 g | Protein: 11.6 g | Sodium: 321 mg
Fiber: 12.6 g | Carbohydrates: 64.8 g | Sugar: 3.3 g

Tempeh Teriyaki Meatball Bites

These Asian-inspired meatballs are filled with protein-rich tempeh and flavored with a sweet and savory teriyaki coating. They make for the perfect cocktail appetizer, but you could also serve them over Asian noodles for a more filling meal. If you want to get a little fancier, you can also sprinkle on some sesame seeds and finely chopped green onion once these bites have finished baking.

Makes 12 meatballs

Recipe Prep Time: *15 minutes*
Recipe Cook Time: *15 minutes*

8 ounces organic tempeh, broken into pieces
¼ cup flaxseed meal
¼ cup bread crumbs
2 medium cloves garlic, peeled and finely chopped
2 tablespoons sesame oil
½ cup plus 1 tablespoon teriyaki sauce, divided

1 Preheat oven to 400°F. Line a 10" × 15" baking sheet with parchment paper.

2 In a food processor or blender, pulse the tempeh, flaxseed meal, bread crumbs, garlic, sesame oil, and 1 tablespoon teriyaki sauce just until ingredients are well mixed. You don't want to make it too smooth, or the meatballs won't have texture. The texture should be crumbly, but moist.

3 Roll the mixture into 1" balls and spread evenly on the prepared baking sheet. Bake 15 minutes, flipping once halfway through cooking time.

4 Heat remaining teriyaki sauce in a medium saucepan until it comes to a light simmer. When meatballs are ready, add to saucepan and gently stir to coat. Serve warm.

Per 1 meatball

Calories: 90 | Fat: 4.8 g | Protein: 5.2 g | Sodium: 552 mg
Fiber: 0.7 g | Carbohydrates: 6.4 g | Sugar: 2.1 g

Tofu "Ricotta" and Mushroom Crostini

Loaded crostini make lovely appetizers, and these bite-sized snacks use an easy protein-filled tofu "ricotta" instead of normal cheese—which makes them animal- and vegan-friendly. This appetizer is topped with sautéed mushrooms, sliced almonds, and fresh thyme, but you can always just make the tofu ricotta and experiment with different toppings of your own.

Makes 20 crostini

Recipe Prep Time: *20 minutes*
Recipe Cook Time: *20 minutes*

½ French baguette

4 tablespoons extra-virgin olive oil, divided

8 ounces organic extra-firm tofu

1½ tablespoons nutritional yeast

1 tablespoon lemon juice

1½ tablespoons filtered water

¼ teaspoon garlic powder

⅛ teaspoon salt

⅛ teaspoon black pepper

2 large cloves garlic, peeled and finely chopped

2 cups sliced button mushrooms

¼ cup sliced raw almonds

1 tablespoon fresh thyme leaves

1 Preheat oven to 350°F. Slice baguette crosswise into ¼" pieces. Place bread on a large baking sheet and brush both sides with olive oil (about 2 tablespoons total). Bake 10 minutes, then rotate the baking sheet and cook 5 minutes more or until bread is crispy and golden.

2 While the crostini is baking, prepare the ricotta. Squeeze out any excess water from the tofu and soak it up using paper towels. Add tofu, yeast, lemon juice, water, garlic powder, salt, and pepper to a food processor or blender and pulse until just smooth. You don't want to blend too much or the ricotta will become more of a purée. Set aside.

3 Heat remaining 2 tablespoons olive oil in a large pan on medium-low. Add garlic and cook 1 minute, stirring occasionally so it doesn't burn. Add mushrooms and sauté 4–5 minutes until softened.

4 Spread ricotta evenly onto crostini. Top with mushrooms, almonds, and thyme. Serve warm.

Per 1 crostini

Calories: 58 | Fat: 3.6 g | Protein: 2.4 g | Sodium: 53 mg
Fiber: 0.5 g | Carbohydrates: 4.3 g | Sugar: 0.6 g

Parmesan-Roasted Chickpeas

If you're someone who likes to nibble on corn nuts or popcorn, you'll love these Parmesan-Roasted Chickpeas. They're baked to crunchy perfection, and they make a great snack to bring to work or school—or to just enjoy while sitting at home watching a movie. If you're vegan or dairy-free, you can always leave out the Parmesan, and the chickpeas will still roast nicely. Or, you can consider using 3 tablespoons of nutritional yeast instead.

Serves 3

Recipe Prep Time: *5 minutes*
Recipe Cook Time: *40 minutes*

- 1 (15-ounce) can chickpeas, rinsed and drained
- 1½ tablespoons extra-virgin olive oil
- ¾ teaspoons garlic powder
- ¼ teaspoon dried oregano
- ¼ teaspoon black pepper
- 3 tablespoons grated Parmesan cheese

1 Pat chickpeas down until they're dry. Add to a large bowl, along with remaining ingredients. Toss until chickpeas are evenly coated.

2 Transfer to a 10" × 15" baking sheet lined with parchment paper and spread out evenly. Bake 20 minutes, and then stir the chickpeas around so they don't burn. Return to oven and cook another 15–20 minutes or until golden and crispy. Let cool slightly before eating.

Per Serving

Calories: 190 | Fat: 8.1 g | Protein: 7.5 g | Sodium: 269 mg
Fiber: 5.5 g | Carbohydrates: 20.8 g | Sugar: 3.4 g

....
TIPS TO MAKE YOUR CHICKPEAS CRISPY

Sometimes it's hard to get your chickpeas perfectly crisped, but the more thoroughly you toss them in the olive oil and the more evenly you spread them on your baking sheet, the crispier they'll get.
....

Super-Green Flatbread with Kale Pistachio Pesto

Flatbreads are easy to make and great for sharing, but they're usually loaded with cheese and lacking in protein. This vegan-friendly flatbread has a Kale Pistachio Pesto base and is topped with chickpeas, which provide some plant-based protein. You can buy a ready-made flatbread from the store, but if one is not available, you can use a large pita or large lavash bread in the same way.

Serves 4

Recipe Prep Time: *15 minutes*
Recipe Cook Time: *10 minutes*

Kale Pistachio Pesto

2 cups fresh kale leaves
2 tablespoons chopped pistachios
2 medium cloves garlic, peeled and finely chopped
2 tablespoons lemon juice
2 tablespoons extra-virgin olive oil

Super-Green Flatbread

1 flatbread
½ small white onion, peeled and cut into small rings
¾ cup baby broccoli
½ cup cooked chickpeas, rinsed and drained
1½ teaspoons olive oil
2 basil leaves, finely sliced

1 Preheat oven to 425°F.

2 **For Kale Pistachio Pesto:** Prepare pesto by blending ingredients together in a blender or food processor on high speed until smooth, about 10–15 seconds.

3 **For Super-Green Flatbread:** Place flatbread on a large baking sheet lined with parchment paper. Spread pesto on the flatbread, leaving about 1" around the border for the crust.

4 Add onion, baby broccoli, and chickpeas to the flatbread. Drizzle with 1½ teaspoons olive oil, and transfer to the oven. Bake 7–10 minutes until flatbread is golden. Top with basil and serve warm.

Per Serving

Calories: 167 | Fat: 8.9 g | Protein: 4.7 g | Sodium: 122 mg
Fiber: 3.7 g | Carbohydrates: 18.0 g | Sugar: 1.9 g

Spinach and Artichoke Dip

Spinach and artichoke dip is usually viewed as an indulgent, unhealthy food, but this version is not only healthy, but it's also rich in protein. It might seem crazy, but there's no cream or cheese in this version. Instead, white beans, cashews, nutritional yeast, and almond milk are blended together to create a creamy, garlicky base that's combined with fresh spinach and artichoke hearts to give you that classic dip flavor—filled with those plant-based proteins that your body craves.

Serves 6

Recipe Prep Time: *30 minutes*
Recipe Cook Time: *11 minutes*

½ cup raw unsalted cashews

1 tablespoon extra-virgin olive oil

½ medium yellow onion, peeled and chopped

4 cups fresh baby spinach leaves

12 ounces chopped artichoke hearts

1 (15-ounce) can cannellini beans, rinsed and drained

½ teaspoon garlic powder

¼ cup nutritional yeast

¾ cup unsweetened almond milk

½ teaspoon salt

1 Bring a small pot of water to boil. Place the cashews in a medium bowl. Cover the cashews with the boiling water; let sit 30 minutes to soften.

2 While cashews are softening, heat olive oil in a large pan on medium heat. Add onion and cook 4–5 minutes until translucent. Add spinach and cook 2 minutes or until spinach begins to wilt, stirring occasionally. Mix in the artichoke, and then remove from heat.

3 In a blender or food processor, blend together soaked cashews, beans, garlic powder, nutritional yeast, almond milk, and salt on high speed until smooth, about 10–20 seconds. Add the mixture to the pan with the spinach and artichokes, and heat on medium to warm the dip, mixing everything together and stirring occasionally. Cook 2–4 minutes or until mixture has thickened. Serve warm.

Per Serving
Calories: 205 | Fat: 8.4 g | Protein: 10.6 g | Sodium: 403 mg
Fiber: 9.7 g | Carbohydrates: 24.6 g | Sugar: 2.0 g

Garlic Chili Edamame

There's nothing like getting a bowl of edamame to nibble on when you're out to dinner at an Asian restaurant. It helps to curb your hunger and it tastes delicious. These in-shell edamame beans are coated in a spicy garlic sauce, and, since they only take about 10 minutes to prepare, they can be enjoyed as a snack before meals or any time throughout the day. If you're not a fan of spicy foods, you can leave out the red pepper flakes, or you can make this dish more mild by using only half of the flakes that the recipe calls for.

Serves 4

Recipe Prep Time: *5 minutes*
Recipe Cook Time: *6 minutes*

6 cups water

12 ounces frozen organic in-shell edamame

2 tablespoons sesame oil

4 medium cloves garlic, peeled and finely chopped

2 tablespoons low-sodium soy sauce

1 teaspoon red pepper flakes

1 Bring water to a boil. Add edamame and cook 4–6 minutes until tender. Drain.

2 While edamame is cooking, heat sesame oil in a medium pan on medium-low heat. Add garlic and cook 1 minute, stirring so it doesn't burn. Mix in soy sauce and red pepper flakes, and cook 1 minute. Remove from heat.

3 Toss edamame in sauce, and serve warm.

Per Serving

Calories: 114 | Fat: 8.6 g | Protein: 5.4 g | Sodium: 255 mg
Fiber: 2.2 g | Carbohydrates: 5.1 g | Sugar: 1.1 g

Curried Chickpea Lettuce Cups

These light but flavorful lettuce cups are both sweet and spicy. Inspired by Indian flavors, the chickpea salad is spiced with curry, cumin, and cayenne pepper and is balanced with some sweetness from the lime and honey. These lettuce cups make a great appetizer or snack on a hot day—or whenever you find yourself looking to add some extra plant-based proteins to your diet.

Makes 4 lettuce cups

Recipe Prep Time: *10 minutes*
Recipe Cook Time: *N/A*

4 butter lettuce leaves
1 (15-ounce) can chickpeas, rinsed and drained
2 tablespoons Vegenaise
1 teaspoon raw wild honey
1 teaspoon extra-virgin olive oil
½ teaspoon curry powder
¼ teaspoon ground cumin
¼ teaspoon cayenne pepper
¼ teaspoon salt
1 tablespoon chopped fresh cilantro
1 tablespoon lime juice

1 Lay butter lettuce flat on a smooth surface.

2 Add chickpeas to a large bowl and smash with a fork. Chickpeas should be mashed, but still remain chunky with some texture. You don't want to make them too smooth or creamy.

3 In a small bowl, combine Vegenaise, honey, olive oil, spices, and salt until smooth. Add the mixture to the chickpeas, along with cilantro and lime juice. Toss everything together until chickpeas are evenly coated and the spice sauce is mixed in.

4 Spoon chickpea mixture into the butter lettuce and serve.

Per 1 lettuce cup

Calories: 150 | Fat: 6.7 g | Protein: 4.7 g | Sodium: 322 mg
Fiber: 4.3 g | Carbohydrates: 17.2 g | Sugar: 4.1 g

Lentil-Stuffed Jalapeño Poppers

Jalapeño poppers are fun party appetizers, and this recipe lets you spruce them up to be more nutritious by adding in some cooked lentils for extra protein. This dish is particularly easy to make when you have extra lentils from the week that you need to put to use. You can also experiment with different cheeses, using feta to make the poppers more Mediterranean-inspired or goat cheese to make the poppers a bit more creamy.

Makes 12 poppers

Recipe Prep Time: *5 minutes*
Recipe Cook Time: *20 minutes*

6 medium jalapeños
⅔ cup cooked green lentils
½ cup shredded Cheddar
  cheese
1 tablespoon extra-virgin
  olive oil

1   Slice jalapeños in half lengthwise. Scoop out the flesh and seeds.
2   Fill the insides of jalapeños with lentils. Top with cheese and olive oil. Bake 15–20 minutes or until cheese is melted and jalapeños have softened.

Per 1 popper

Calories: 43 | Fat: 2.5 g | Protein: 2.2 g | Sodium: 30 mg
Fiber: 1.2 g | Carbohydrates: 2.7 g | Sugar: 0.5 g

....

GET OUT THOSE GLOVES

When cutting open the jalapeños and scooping out the flesh and seeds, be sure to wear gloves to protect your hands from the spicy juices. If you touch the jalapeños and then touch your face, or worse, your nose or eyes, you're in for a painful burn!

....

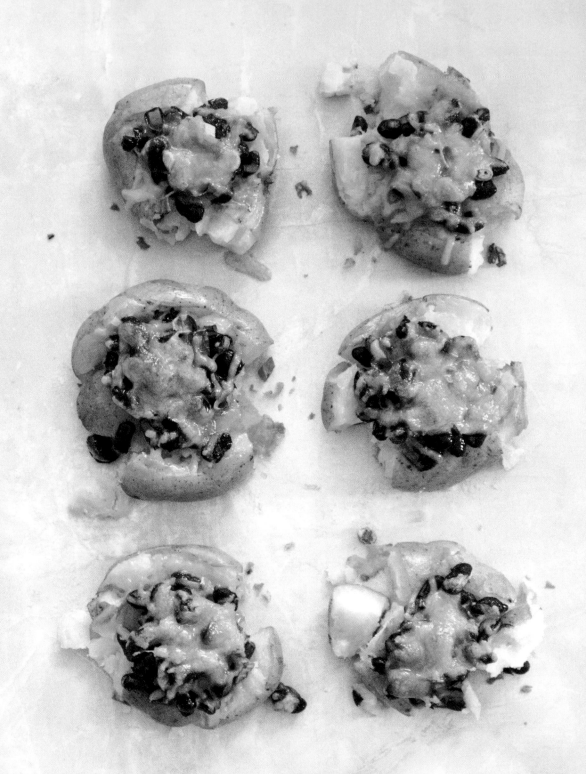

Loaded Smashed Potatoes

On those days when you're sick of eating mashed or baked potatoes, mix things up and eat these Loaded Smashed Potatoes instead. They're soft on the inside, crisp on the outside, and loaded with protein-filled kidney beans, melted Cheddar cheese, and green onion. Russet potatoes won't work here, as they're too big, so make sure you buy Yukon gold potatoes instead.

Serves 6

Recipe Prep Time: *5 minutes*
Recipe Cook Time: *50 minutes*

6 medium Yukon gold potatoes (unpeeled)

3 tablespoons extra-virgin olive oil

1 (15-ounce) can kidney beans, rinsed and drained

1 medium green onion, finely chopped

¾ cup shredded Cheddar cheese

¼ teaspoon salt

1 Preheat oven to 450°F. Line a 10" × 15" baking sheet with aluminum foil.

2 Add potatoes to a large pot and cover with water. Bring to a boil over medium-high heat and cook 35–40 minutes until potatoes are tender.

3 Drain potatoes and transfer to the prepared baking sheet. Lightly smash the potatoes with a potato masher or the back of a glass. Top each potato with oil, beans, onion, and Cheddar. Bake 10 minutes or until cheese starts to get crispy. Top with salt and serve warm.

Per Serving

Calories: 321 | Fat: 11.2 g | Protein: 11.2 g | Sodium: 321 mg
Fiber: 7.1 g | Carbohydrates: 43.7 g | Sugar: 2.8 g

Almond Mint Pea Dip

You've probably eaten your weight in guacamole and bean dip over the course of your lifetime, but these aren't the only dips you can enjoy with some chips. Try your hand at this amazing Almond Mint Pea Dip, which is loaded with protein thanks to the peas and almonds. Spread it on a cracker, eat it with some carrots, or add it to a sandwich—no matter how you eat it, this pea dip will add a refreshing twist.

Makes 2 cups

Recipe Prep Time: *10 minutes*
Recipe Cook Time: *5 minutes*

2 cups frozen peas
½ cup raw sliced almonds
¼ cup fresh mint leaves
2 medium cloves garlic,
    peeled and chopped
Juice of 2 small lemons
¼ teaspoon salt

1 Bring a medium pot of water to a boil; add peas and cook 2–3 minutes until soft. Drain and rinse with cold water.

2 Add peas, almonds, mint, garlic, and lemon to a blender or food processor and blend on high speed until ingredients are combined, about 10–20 seconds. Texture should be thick and chunky. Mix in salt. Serve immediately or keep refrigerated. Dip will last up to 3 days.

Per ¼ cup serving

Calories: 69 | Fat: 2.8 g | Protein: 3.5 g | Sodium: 74 mg
Fiber: 3.0 g | Carbohydrates: 8.1 g | Sugar: 2.7 g

Quinoa-Stuffed Tomatoes

Stuffed tomatoes sound tough to make, but they're actually quite simple to prepare. Look for tomatoes that are only medium-ripe, because you don't want them to be so soft that they fall apart. The stuffing, which contains protein from the quinoa and walnuts, is vegan-friendly, but if you want to add a sprinkle of cheese on top, add some during the last 5 minutes of baking so it doesn't get too crispy in the oven.

Makes 6 tomatoes

Recipe Prep Time: *10 minutes*
Recipe Cook Time: *20 minutes*

½ cup quinoa
1 cup water
6 medium on-the-vine tomatoes
1 tablespoon extra-virgin olive oil
1 medium yellow onion, peeled and chopped
4 medium cloves garlic, peeled and finely chopped
½ cup finely chopped raw walnuts
⅓ cup chopped fresh Italian flat-leaf parsley
¼ teaspoon salt

1 Preheat oven to 375°F. Line a 10" × 15" baking sheet with aluminum foil.

2 Cook quinoa according to package instructions.

3 While quinoa is cooking, prepare tomatoes. Slice off the top of the tomatoes, and use a knife to scoop out the inside so it's hollow. Place tomatoes on the prepared baking sheet so that they're sitting upright. Set aside.

4 Add olive oil to a large pan on medium-low heat. Add onions and garlic, and cook 3–4 minutes until onions are translucent. Add cooked quinoa to the pan, along with walnuts, parsley, and salt, and mix together. Remove from heat.

5 Scoop the quinoa mixture evenly into each tomato. Bake 15 minutes. Serve warm.

Per 1 stuffed tomato

Calories: 153 | Fat: 9.1 g | Protein: 4.2 g | Sodium: 100 mg
Fiber: 2.6 g | Carbohydrates: 14.5 g | Sugar: 2.3 g

Plant-Protein Guacamole

It's hard to find someone who doesn't love guacamole, but it's not exactly the best source of protein. Thankfully, this recipe solves that problem. The puréed edamame and chia seeds found in this dish give this appetizer a protein boost without compromising taste. This guacamole is perfect with corn chips, or you can add it to foods like tacos and chili.

Serves 6

Recipe Prep Time: *20 minutes*
Recipe Cook Time: *N/A*

2 large ripe avocados

4 teaspoons lime juice (about 2 limes)

1 cup frozen shelled edamame, thawed

2 tablespoons chopped fresh cilantro

¼ cup finely chopped red onion

½ medium jalapeño, seeded and finely chopped

3 tablespoons chia seeds

¼ teaspoon salt

1 Cut the avocados in half and remove the pits. Scoop out the flesh and place it in a large bowl. Add the lime juice, and toss to coat.

2 Add edamame to a blender or food processor and blend on high speed until a purée has formed, about 10–20 seconds. Add the purée to the bowl with the avocado and mash together with a fork until smooth.

3 Fold in the cilantro, onion, jalapeño, chia seeds, and salt. Serve immediately.

Per Serving

Calories: 146 | Fat: 9.7 g | Protein: 6.4 g | Sodium: 101 mg
Fiber: 6.2 g | Carbohydrates: 9.3 g | Sugar: 1.4 g

STORING THE GUAC

Guacamole is best served fresh, but if you have to store it for later, make sure you cover it in either plastic wrap or aluminum foil. Also, squeeze some lemon on top to help prevent the avocado from oxidizing.

Buffalo Tempeh Wings

Impress your friends with these game day–ready vegan buffalo wings! Thanks to the tempeh, this dish contains plenty of protein, but the buffalo sauce helps it retain that signature spicy kick that you expect to find when you bite into a wing. This recipe uses mild buffalo sauce, but you can always use a spicier version if you'd like. This dish make 6 generous-sized wings for a hearty appetizer, but you can cut the tempeh strips a little smaller if you want to serve bite-sized snacks instead.

Makes 6 wings

Recipe Prep Time: *15 minutes*
Recipe Cook Time: *23 minutes*

8 ounces organic tempeh, cut into 1¼" strips
1 cup buffalo sauce, divided
¼ cup whole-wheat flour
¼ cup bread crumbs
¼ teaspoon paprika
⅛ teaspoon garlic powder
⅛ teaspoon cayenne pepper

1. Preheat oven to 400°F. Bring a medium pot of water to a boil. Add tempeh and boil 5 minutes. Remove tempeh from water and add to a plastic zipper bag filled with ½ cup buffalo sauce. Let marinate 15 minutes.

2. While tempeh is marinating, combine flour, bread crumbs, paprika, garlic powder, and cayenne pepper in a medium bowl.

3. Line a 10" × 15" baking sheet with parchment paper. Dip each tempeh slice into the flour mix, coating both sides, and spread out the dipped tempeh strips evenly on baking sheet. Bake 15 minutes.

4. Remove wings from the oven, and brush the remaining ½ cup buffalo sauce onto the wings, coating both sides. Bake 2–3 more minutes, and serve warm.

Per 2 wings

Calories: 218 | Fat: 7.5 g | Protein: 16.8 g | Sodium: 1,980 mg
Fiber: 1.7 g | Carbohydrates: 21.4 g | Sugar: 0.7 g

Quinoa Cakes with Mango Salsa

The proteins in these lightly-fried quinoa cakes make this dish filling, but it is topped with a light and tropical mango salsa that won't leave you feeling weighed down. Since these cakes are made with quinoa, potato, and almond flour, they are gluten-free, and they are also dairy- and egg-free, which makes them perfect for vegans too.

Makes 8 quinoa cakes

Recipe Prep Time: *15 minutes*
Recipe Cook Time: *23 minutes*

1 cup quinoa

2 cups water

1 cup chopped mango

½ cup peeled and chopped red onion

2 tablespoons finely chopped fresh cilantro

Juice of 1 lime

1 cup grated russet potatoes

½ cup almond flour

1 large green onion, thinly sliced

2 large cloves garlic, peeled and minced

½ cup avocado oil

½ teaspoon black pepper

½ teaspoon salt

1 Add quinoa and water to a medium saucepan and bring to a boil. Reduce to a simmer, cover, and cook until all the water is absorbed, about 10–15 minutes.

2 While quinoa is cooking, prepare the mango salsa by mixing together mango, onion, cilantro, and lime juice in a small bowl; set aside.

3 Add quinoa to a large bowl along with grated potato, almond flour, green onion, and garlic. Mix until everything is evenly combined. Form the mixture into 8 equal-sized round cakes.

4 Heat oil in a large skillet on medium heat. Gently place the patties in the pan with a spatula. Cook 4 minutes on each side. Remove from pan, letting excess oil drip out, and place in between paper towels to soak up oil. Season with pepper and salt. Top with mango salsa and serve immediately.

Per 1 cake

Calories: 205 | Fat: 10.5 g | Protein: 3.8 g | Sodium: 147 mg
Fiber: 3.1 g | Carbohydrates: 23.1 g | Sugar: 3.4 g

DON'T USE OLIVE OIL TO FRY

Whenever you're frying something on a higher heat, avoid using olive oil, as it has a lower smoke point and can burn easily. Instead, use an oil with a higher smoking point such as avocado oil, vegetable oil, or grapeseed oil.

Spicy Quinoa Vegetable Hand Rolls

Hand rolls might seem intimidating to make, but they are actually fairly easy—and you don't have to include any raw fish to make them taste good. This fiery, protein-filled appetizer is filled with quinoa, vegetables, avocado, and seeds, as well as sriracha for a kick of spiciness. Once you start rolling, you might be surprised at how quickly you pick up on it.

Makes 6 hand rolls

Recipe Prep Time: *15 minutes*
Recipe Cook Time: *N/A*

1 cup cooked quinoa

¼ cup rice vinegar

3 sheets nori (seaweed)

1 large peeled carrot

½ peeled English cucumber

½ medium avocado, peeled and sliced

2 teaspoons sriracha

1 tablespoon hemp seeds

1 tablespoon sesame seeds

1 Combine quinoa and vinegar in a medium bowl, mixing evenly until quinoa is sticky.

2 Lay seaweed sheets flat, shiny side facing down. On the left side of your seaweed sheet, spoon about 3 tablespoons quinoa evenly onto each sheet, pressing flat.

3 Slice carrots and cucumbers thinly lengthwise and then again crosswise so you have very thin slices. Place those on top of the quinoa. Add the avocado slices, sriracha, hemp seeds, and sesame seeds.

4 To fold up hand rolls, take the left corner and begin to roll up diagonally into a cone shape, tucking the seaweed in as you go to secure. Serve immediately.

Per 1 hand roll

Calories: 84 | Fat: 3.6 g | Protein: 2.7 g | Sodium: 38 mg
Fiber: 2.3 g | Carbohydrates: 10.0 g | Sugar: 1.5 g

CHAPTER 7

SIDE DISHES

"Macaroni and Cheese" with Spinach and Tomatoes

If you're going to eat pasta, you want to ditch the white, refined wheat version and opt for a more protein-filled version such as a black bean pasta, quinoa pasta, or lentil pasta. The lentil pasta used in this dish is available at many grocery stores, and it's a great way to enjoy a comfort dish while still getting in all your nutrients. The flavor of this "mac and cheese" is mild, and the texture is very similar to regular pasta. The "cheese" used here is completely dairy-free and vegan, and adds some protein from the cashews.

Serves 2

Recipe Prep Time: *30 minutes*
Recipe Cook Time: *10 minutes*

2 cups dry lentil rotini pasta

2 tablespoons extra-virgin olive oil, divided

2 cups fresh spinach leaves

½ cup raw unsalted cashews

4 medium cloves garlic, peeled and finely chopped

½ cup plus 2 tablespoons filtered water

½ teaspoon salt

½ teaspoon black pepper

½ cup halved cherry tomatoes

1 Prepare pasta according to package directions. Rinse and drain.

2 In a medium pan, heat 1 tablespoon olive oil on medium-low. Add spinach leaves and cook 1–2 minutes until wilted. Remove from heat.

3 In a blender or food processor, blend together cashews, garlic, water, 1 tablespoon olive oil, salt, and pepper on high speed until completely smooth, about 10–20 seconds.

4 Return pasta to pot and add sauce. Mix together on low heat; cook about 2–3 minutes until sauce is warm and thick. Fold in spinach and cherry tomatoes, and serve warm.

Per Serving

Calories: 693 | Fat: 29.8 g | Protein: 32.5 g | Sodium: 611 mg
Fiber: 24.0 g | Carbohydrates: 84.3 g | Sugar: 3.4 g

Roasted Cauliflower and Chickpeas

The roasted cauliflower used in this dish is softer, sweeter, and much more palatable than raw cauliflower. When chickpeas are roasted, however, they get nice and crispy, and the juxtaposition of these two main ingredients makes for an interesting, multitextured side dish. Don't be surprised when your family and friends ask you to make this side whenever you invite them over for dinner. It's just that delicious!

Serves 4

Recipe Prep Time: *10 minutes*
Recipe Cook Time: *40 minutes*

1 head cauliflower, cut into bite-sized florets
1 (15-ounce) can chickpeas, rinsed and drained
¼ cup extra-virgin olive oil
¼ teaspoon salt
¼ teaspoon black pepper
½ tablespoon Dijon mustard
2 medium cloves garlic, peeled and minced
Juice of 2 small lemons
1 tablespoon white vinegar
¼ teaspoon red pepper flakes
2 tablespoons chopped fresh Italian flat-leaf parsley

1 Preheat oven to 425°F. In a large bowl, toss together cauliflower, chickpeas, olive oil, salt, and pepper. Spread mixture evenly on a large roasting pan, and bake 30–40 minutes until cauliflower has started to turn golden and crisp and chickpeas are crispy.

2 While cauliflower and chickpeas are roasting, combine mustard, garlic, lemon juice, and vinegar in a small bowl.

3 Toss cauliflower and chickpeas with the mustard mixture along with red pepper flakes and parsley until everything is evenly coated. Serve warm.

Per Serving
Calories: 209 | Fat: 11.7 g | Protein: 6.2 g | Sodium: 315 mg
Fiber: 5.8 g | Carbohydrates: 34.0 g | Sugar: 4.5 g

Peas and Potatoes with Spinach Almond Pesto

Peas and potatoes are two vegetables with some of the highest protein content. Put them together, and you have a side dish that everyone will love! These protein-packed potatoes and peas are tossed in almond, spinach, and basil-based pesto, which not only give the dish a creamy consistency, but adds even more protein, thanks to the almonds.

Serves 6

Recipe Prep Time: *10 minutes*
Recipe Cook Time: *25 minutes*

1½ pounds baby yellow potatoes

1 tablespoon extra-virgin olive oil

1 pound frozen peas

Zest of 2 lemons (you can use same ones you will use for pesto)

Spinach Almond Pesto

½ cup raw sliced almonds

4 medium cloves garlic, peeled and roughly chopped

2 cups fresh spinach leaves

1 cup fresh basil leaves

Juice of 2 small lemons

2 tablespoons olive oil

¼ cup filtered water

¼ teaspoon salt

1 Add potatoes to a large pot and cover with cold water. Bring to a boil, reduce to a simmer, and cook 20–25 minutes until potatoes are tender.

2 Meanwhile, heat 1 tablespoon olive oil in a medium pan over medium heat. Add peas and lemon zest, and cook 5 minutes or until peas begin to soften.

3 **For Spinach Almond Pesto:** Add all ingredients except the water and salt to a food processor or blender. Blend on high speed 10–20 seconds until the pesto is smooth. Once the pesto is smooth, mix in the water along with salt.

4 Combine potatoes and peas in a large bowl. Toss with pesto and serve warm, or refrigerate and serve chilled.

Per Serving

Calories: 244 | Fat: 10.0 g | Protein: 8.1 g | Sodium: 204 mg
Fiber: 7.7 g | Carbohydrates: 24.0 g | Sugar: 5.8 g

Asian Peanut Noodles with Edamame

Don't freak out when you get that craving for greasy takeout! Just make your own Asian noodles at home without any of that unhealthy MSG or added salt. This noodle dish gets its protein—and some of it's delicious flavors—from the brown rice noodles, peanut butter sauce, and shelled edamame. These noodles are fairly mild, but you can make them spicier by adding in an extra ½ teaspoon red pepper flakes.

Serves 6

Recipe Prep Time: *20 minutes*
Recipe Cook Time: *10 minutes*

8 ounces brown rice noodles

2 tablespoons sesame oil

½ teaspoon red pepper flakes

3 tablespoons low-sodium soy sauce

½ cup raw creamy peanut butter

1 tablespoon apple cider vinegar

¼ teaspoon garlic powder

12 ounces cooked organic shelled edamame

2 small green onions, thinly sliced

1 Prepare pasta according to package instructions.

2 In a large pan, heat sesame oil on medium-low. Add red pepper flakes, and stir 1 minute. Mix in soy sauce, peanut butter, vinegar, and garlic powder. Stir until combined, and remove from heat.

3 Toss noodles with sauce and edamame, and top with green onion. Serve warm, or chill and serve cold.

___

Per Serving

Calories: 410 | Fat: 21.4 g | Protein: 19.8 g | Sodium: 256 mg
Fiber: 7.7 g | Carbohydrates: 36.9 g | Sugar: 3.1 g

Spicy Black Pepper Tofu

This tofu dish is inspired by Israeli chef Yotam Ottolenghi, who really knows how to get creative with plant-based cooking. The tofu gets its spiciness from the black pepper and red pepper flakes, but this heat is balanced out by the sweetness of the honey and the cooked-down garlic and shallots. This Spicy Black Pepper Tofu is great as a side dish on it's own, but it can also be served with rice or quinoa or some vegetables to make it a more complete meal.

Serves 4

Recipe Prep Time: *15 minutes*
Recipe Cook Time: *22 minutes*

- 1 pound organic extra-firm tofu
- ¼ cup sesame oil
- 1 large shallot, peeled and finely chopped
- 8 medium cloves garlic, peeled and minced
- ¼ teaspoon red pepper flakes
- 2 tablespoons low-sodium soy sauce
- ½ tablespoon raw wild honey
- 1 teaspoon black pepper
- ⅓ cup thinly sliced green onion

1 Cut tofu into 1" cubes. In a large pan heat sesame oil on medium heat and add tofu. Fry tofu about 10 minutes, turning it occasionally so it cooks evenly. Once tofu has turned golden, remove it from the pan and set aside on a paper towel.

2 In the same pan, stir together shallots, garlic, and red pepper flakes and lower the heat to medium-low. Cook 10 minutes, stirring frequently until shallots soften. Add soy sauce and honey, stirring until evenly mixed. Add black pepper.

3 Add tofu and cook 1–2 minutes until heated through. Mix in the green onions, and serve warm.

Per Serving

Calories: 262 | Fat: 19.3 g | Protein: 13.0 g | Sodium: 268 mg
Fiber: 1.7 g | Carbohydrates: 11.2 g | Sugar: 4.6 g

"Cheesy" Crispy Brussels Sprouts

Roasted Brussels sprouts are good, but *cheesy* Brussels sprouts are even better. This recipe uses nutritional yeast and tahini as "cheese," which not only eliminates the need for dairy, but adds a dose of protein to the dish as well. So say goodbye to the days of eating plain, boiled, and bitter vegetables and get ready to nibble on these protein-packed sprouts instead.

Serves 4

Recipe Prep Time: *10 minutes*
Recipe Cook Time: *15 minutes*

4 cups shaved Brussels sprouts
⅓ cup nutritional yeast
2 tablespoons tahini
1 teaspoon garlic powder
¼ teaspoon salt

1 Preheat oven to 375°F. Add Brussels sprouts to a large bowl.

2 Blend together yeast, tahini, garlic powder, and salt in a food processor or blender on high until smooth, about 20–30 seconds. Add the nutritional yeast blend to the Brussels sprouts and use your hands to massage it into the sprouts until they're evenly coated.

3 Line a 10" × 15" baking sheet with aluminum foil. Spread Brussels sprouts evenly onto the sheet, making sure they're in a single layer. Bake 10 minutes, and then broil on high 2–5 minutes until crispy. Check at the 2-minute mark to see if the edges of the Brussels sprouts are crispy. If not, broil 2–3 minutes more.

Per Serving

Calories: 104 | Fat: 4.2 g | Protein: 7.0 g | Sodium: 184 mg
Fiber: 5.1 g | Carbohydrates: 11.7 g | Sugar: 2.0 g

Jamaican-Inspired Rice and Beans

This rice dish is inspired by the classic Jamaican meal "Rice and Peas." Don't be fooled though—there are no peas in this dish. In Jamaica, kidney beans are referred to as peas, and in this hearty side dish, they're cooked with brown rice, coconut milk, onions, garlic, and spices like thyme and paprika that you likely already have on hand.

Serves 8

Recipe Prep Time: *15 minutes*
Recipe Cook Time: *30 minutes*

- 2 tablespoons extra-virgin olive oil
- 4 medium cloves garlic, peeled and finely chopped
- ½ medium yellow onion, peeled and chopped
- 2 cups uncooked long-grain brown rice
- 1 (13.5-ounce) can coconut milk
- 2 cups water
- 1 teaspoon ground allspice
- 1 teaspoon dried thyme
- 1 teaspoon paprika
- ¼ teaspoon salt
- 1 (15-ounce) can kidney beans, rinsed and drained

1 Heat 1 tablespoon olive oil in a medium saucepan on medium-low. Add garlic and onions. Cook about 4 minutes, stirring occasionally until onions are translucent.

2 Stir in brown rice and cook 1 minute. Add coconut milk, water, allspice, thyme, paprika, and salt, and stir together. Bring to a boil, and then reduce heat to a simmer. Cover and cook 15 minutes. Mix in kidney beans, cover, and cook 10–15 minutes or until liquid is absorbed.

Per Serving

Calories: 342 | Fat: 14.4 g | Protein: 7.7 g | Sodium: 154 mg
Fiber: 4.5 g | Carbohydrates: 45.7 g | Sugar: 0.7 g

Pistachio-and-Hemp-Seed-Crusted Root Vegetables

Don't let those leftover vegetables sit in your refrigerator and go bad. Instead, throw them into the oven and roast them to create this protein-packed side dish! Roasted vegetables become soft and tender when cooked this way, and you can either eat them right then and there as a side or save them later for a bowl or salad.

Serves 4

Recipe Prep Time: *15 minutes*
Recipe Cook Time: *25 minutes*

1 medium sweet potato
1 medium russet potato
2 medium beets
6 medium multicolored carrots
½ cup raw pistachios
3 tablespoons hemp seeds
¼ teaspoon salt
2½ tablespoons extra-virgin olive oil
3 tablespoons fresh thyme leaves

1 Preheat oven to 425°F. Slice sweet potato, potato, and beets crosswise into thin ½" slices. Spread evenly onto 2 large baking sheets in single layers. Cut carrots diagonally into 1" pieces. Add to baking sheet, or a separate baking sheet if needed.

2 Pulse pistachios in a food processor or blender just 1–2 seconds to crush. You don't want to pulse for too long or the pistachios will turn into a powder. Add to a small bowl, and mix in hemp seeds and salt.

3 Drizzle olive oil evenly over vegetables. Sprinkle on the pistachio mixture, and top off with thyme. Bake 25 minutes or until vegetables are soft. Let vegetables cool 5 minutes, and then mix together in a large bowl. Serve warm.

Per Serving

Calories: 344 | Fat: 16.8 g | Protein: 9.9 g | Sodium: 259 mg
Fiber: 7.8 g | Carbohydrates: 40.6 g | Sugar: 10.0 g

Roasted Broccoli with Almonds

You may have hated broccoli growing up, but once you try this dish, you'll find yourself changing your mind about this cruciferous vegetable. Roasting the broccoli makes it more tender and less bitter, and adding in a little lemon, Parmesan cheese, and red pepper flakes adds some tanginess, saltiness, and spiciness to this plant-based side dish.

Serves 4

Recipe Prep Time: 10 minutes
Recipe Cook Time: 25 minutes

2 heads broccoli (about 1½ pounds), cut into medium florets

¼ cup extra-virgin olive oil

¼ teaspoon red pepper flakes

¼ teaspoon black pepper

3 tablespoons sliced raw almonds

3 tablespoons shaved Parmesan cheese

Juice of 1 small lemon

1 Preheat oven to 450°F. Line a 10" × 15" baking sheet with aluminum foil.

2 Add broccoli to a large bowl along with olive oil, red pepper flakes, and black pepper, and toss until broccoli is evenly coated.

3 Spread broccoli on the prepared baking sheet. Bake 10 minutes, then flip broccoli and sprinkle almonds on top. Bake another 10–15 minutes until broccoli is tender. Add to a bowl and toss with Parmesan and lemon juice. Serve warm.

Per Serving

Calories: 199 | Fat: 13.7 g | Protein: 7.5 g | Sodium: 123 mg
Fiber: 5.4 g | Carbohydrates: 13.9 g | Sugar: 3.5 g

Deconstructed Pesto Quinoa

This quinoa is perfect for the days when you feel like having all the flavors of pesto, but can't bring yourself to take out your blender or food processor. In this dish the protein-rich quinoa is tossed with all the ingredients of your typical pesto: pine nuts (for more protein), basil, Parmesan cheese, garlic, and olive oil. You still get the herby, pungent taste of pesto, but you don't have to go through the hassle of making it first.

Serves 4

Recipe Prep Time: *10 minutes*
Recipe Cook Time: *15 minutes*

1 cup quinoa
2 cups water
½ cup toasted pine nuts
¼ cup chopped fresh basil
½ cup grated Parmesan cheese
2 large cloves garlic, peeled and minced
Juice of 3 small lemons
3 tablespoons extra-virgin olive oil

1 Add quinoa and water to a medium saucepan and bring to a boil. Reduce to a simmer, cover, and cook until quinoa is soft and all the water is absorbed, 10–15 minutes. Let quinoa cool 15 minutes.

2 Add quinoa to a large bowl along with remaining ingredients. Toss until well mixed. Serve warm or chilled.

Per Serving

Calories: 419 | Fat: 25.0 g | Protein: 12.1 g | Sodium: 228 mg
Fiber: 3.7 g | Carbohydrates: 33.3 g | Sugar: 1.2 g

Roasted Carrots and Chickpeas with Harissa

The combination of carrots and chickpeas along with harissa topping in this dish is influenced by the flavors of North Africa, which commonly include a blend of sweet and savory flavors along with a variety of spices. While roasting the carrots makes them softer and sweeter, roasting the chickpeas gives them a little crunch, which makes for a nice contrasting texture in each bite.

Serves 6

Recipe Prep Time: *15 minutes*
Recipe Cook Time: *50 minutes*

- 6 medium carrots, sliced in half lengthwise
- 1 (15-ounce) can chickpeas, rinsed and drained
- 2½ tablespoons extra-virgin olive oil
- ½ teaspoon dried oregano
- ¼ teaspoon dried thyme
- ½ teaspoon ground cumin
- ¼ teaspoon salt
- ¼ teaspoon black pepper

Harissa

- 2 tablespoons no-salt-added tomato paste
- 2 medium cloves garlic, peeled and finely chopped
- 1 tablespoon chili powder
- 1 tablespoon ground cumin
- ½ teaspoon paprika
- ½ teaspoon ground caraway
- 1 tablespoon lemon juice
- ⅓ cup extra-virgin olive oil

1 Preheat oven to 450°F. Add sliced carrots to a 6" × 10" baking dish. Pat chickpeas dry with a paper towel and add them to the pan, spreading them evenly over and around the carrots.

2 Drizzle carrots and chickpeas with olive oil, and top with oregano, thyme, cumin, salt, and pepper. Bake 45–50 minutes or until chickpeas are crispy and carrots are soft.

3 **For Harissa:** Meanwhile, prepare harissa by combining all ingredients in a small bowl and mixing until smooth.

4 Top carrots and chickpeas with harissa, and serve warm.

Per Serving

Calories: 243 | Fat: 17.3 g | Protein: 4.3 g | Sodium: 269 mg
Fiber: 5.3 g | Carbohydrates: 18.3 g | Sugar: 5.3 g

Lemon Broccoli Rabe and White Beans

If you're sick of eating the same old sautéed greens, give broccoli rabe a try every so often. Also known as rapini, broccoli rabe has a slightly bitter taste and a unique texture that's different than that of kale or spinach, thanks to its edible leaves, buds, and stems. This side dish is prepared with white beans for protein, and it's seasoned with garlic, lemon, and black pepper that give it a simple but refreshing flavor.

Serves 4

Recipe Prep Time: *10 minutes*
Recipe Cook Time: *7 minutes*

2 tablespoons extra-virgin olive oil

4 small cloves garlic, peeled and minced

1 large bunch broccoli rabe, tough stems removed

Zest and juice of 2 small lemons

1 cup canned white cannellini beans (rinsed and drained)

¼ teaspoon black pepper

1 Heat olive oil in a large pan on medium-low heat. Add garlic and cook about 1 minute, stirring occasionally so it doesn't burn.

2 Add broccoli rabe and lemon zest; cook about 6 minutes until tender and bright green, stirring occasionally so the broccoli cooks evenly.

3 Remove from heat and mix in lemon juice and white beans. Top with black pepper, and serve warm.

Per Serving

Calories: 145 | Fat: 5.4 g | Protein: 8.3 g | Sodium: 61 mg
Fiber: 6.2 g | Carbohydrates: 15.9 g | Sugar: 1.3 g

Deconstructed Mexican Street-Style Corn

Mexican street corn, also known as *elote*, is typically served on the cob with condiments such as butter, mayonnaise, sour cream, lemon or lime juice, and chili powder. This version is served off the cob, so it's easier to serve to multiple people, and it's lightened up to be a bit healthier. Here you'll find that olive oil replaces butter, and Greek yogurt stands in for mayonnaise and sour cream. However, you will find Cotija cheese used here to keep that classic Mexican flavor intact.

Serves 4

Recipe Prep Time: *5 minutes*
Recipe Cook Time: *5 minutes*

2 tablespoons extra-virgin olive oil

4 cups frozen whole yellow corn kernels

¼ cup plain 2% Greek yogurt

½ teaspoon chili powder

½ cup crumbled Cotija cheese

2 tablespoons lime juice

½ teaspoon cayenne pepper

1 teaspoon finely chopped fresh cilantro

1   Add olive oil to a large pan on medium heat. Add corn and cook 4–5 minutes until softened.

2   Transfer to a medium bowl and toss with yogurt, chili powder, Cotija, and lime juice until evenly coated. Top with cayenne pepper and cilantro.

Per Serving

Calories: 274 | Fat: 10.5 g | Protein: 9.9 g | Sodium: 232 mg
Fiber: 4.8 g | Carbohydrates: 40.9 g | Sugar: 7.0 g

USES FOR LEFTOVER CORN

It might be hard to stop yourself from eating all of this street-style corn, but if you do happen to have leftovers, use the corn as a taco or burrito topping, add it to salads, or even toss it in with pasta.

Lentils with Caramelized Onions and Mushrooms

This simple side dish is inspired by the Lebanese lentil-based dish mujadara, which consists of lentils and caramelized onions. If you're vegan, you can always substitute the ghee with more olive oil, but if you want a richer flavor, the ghee adds some creaminess to the dish. You can use these leftovers in salads, wraps, or even in an omelet.

Serves 6

Recipe Prep Time: *10 minutes*
Recipe Cook Time: *40 minutes*

1 cup dried green lentils

2½ cups water

1 teaspoon ghee

1 teaspoon plus 1 tablespoon extra-virgin olive oil, divided

2 medium yellow onions, peeled and sliced

8 ounces button mushrooms, sliced

½ teaspoon salt

⅛ teaspoon black pepper

MAKING THE BEST CARAMELIZED ONIONS

The key to making caramelized onions is patience—they just take some time. You also want to make sure to add any olive oil, butter, or water if the onions start getting too dry, as this will keep them from burning and will allow them to stay moist enough to caramelize. Add about 1 teaspoon at a time, as needed.

1 In a medium pot, combine lentils and water and bring to a boil over medium-high heat. Reduce to a simmer, cover, and cook 35–40 minutes until lentils are tender and most of the liquid is absorbed.

2 Meanwhile, add ghee and 1 teaspoon oil to a large sauté pan over medium heat. Add onions and coat with the ghee mixture. Cook 35–40 minutes, stirring every 10 minutes, until onions are caramelized. They should be brown and soft. If the onions get too dry, add a bit of water.

3 While the lentils and onions are cooking, prepare mushrooms. Add remaining 1 tablespoon olive oil to a large pan on medium heat. Add mushrooms and cook 7–10 minutes until softened. Remove from heat and set aside.

4 Add the cooked lentils and mushrooms to the pan with the onions and reduce heat to low. Add salt and pepper, and mix well. Serve warm.

Per Serving

Calories: 162 | Fat: 3.6 g | Protein: 9.4 g | Sodium: 198 mg
Fiber: 4.4 g | Carbohydrates: 24.6 g | Sugar: 2.8 g

Protein-Packed Mashed Potatoes

You may be wondering how mashed potatoes could possibly be a good source of protein, but these potatoes contain a special ingredient that makes them much more nutritious: white beans. The beans blend seamlessly into the potatoes, so you won't even know they're in there, but they make this side dish much more protein-rich by adding about four grams of protein per serving.

Serves 6

Recipe Prep Time: *5 minutes*
Recipe Cook Time: *20 minutes*

3 pounds Yukon gold potatoes (unpeeled)
1 (15-ounce) can white beans, rinsed and drained
¼ cup nutritional yeast
2 teaspoons garlic powder
½ cup unsweetened almond milk
¼ cup melted ghee
¼ cup finely chopped fresh chives
½ teaspoon salt

1 Add potatoes to a large pot, cover with water, and bring to a boil. Boil 15–20 minutes or until potatoes are tender.

2 While potatoes are cooking, blend together beans, yeast, garlic powder, and almond milk in a blender or food processor on high speed until smooth, about 10–20 seconds.

3 Add drained potatoes to a large bowl. Mash with a potato masher or a fork. Mix in white bean sauce, ghee, chives, and salt until evenly mixed. Serve warm.

Per Serving

Calories: 336 | Fat: 10.6 g | Protein: 11.1 g | Sodium: 252 mg
Fiber: 7.8 g | Carbohydrates: 50.3 g | Sugar: 2.9 g

Soba Noodles with Ginger-Lime Tahini Sauce

This Asian-inspired noodle dish is incredibly refreshing and packed with protein-filled, fresh ingredients. Here the spinach is sautéed and added to the noodles along with cucumber, radish, and kale microgreens, which makes this dish perfect for veggie-lovers. If you're looking to really pack in the nutrients, you'll want to get noodles that are 100 percent buckwheat, which are higher in fiber and protein than regular soba noodles. And, if you're so inclined, you can also make extra of the protein-filled tahini sauce and drizzle it over other dishes for added protein and flavor.

Serves 4

Recipe Prep Time: *30 minutes*
Recipe Cook Time: *10 minutes*

Ginger-Lime Tahini Sauce

¼ cup tahini

2 tablespoons low-sodium soy sauce

¼ cup lime juice

1 tablespoon finely minced ginger

2 tablespoons filtered water

Soba Noodles

8 ounces soba noodles

1 tablespoon sesame oil

6 cups fresh spinach leaves

1 medium Persian cucumber, thinly sliced crosswise

4 radishes, thinly sliced

¼ cup kale microgreens

¼ teaspoon red pepper flakes

1. **For Ginger-Lime Tahini Sauce:** Whisk together all ingredients in a small bowl until smooth. The sauce should be runny enough to drizzle, but if it's not, add more water 1 tablespoon at a time until you get the right consistency.

2. **For Soba Noodles:** Prepare noodles according to package.

3. While noodles are cooking, heat sesame oil in a large pan on medium-low. Add spinach and cook 2 minutes or until wilted.

4. Add noodles and tahini sauce to the pan with the spinach. Toss until evenly coated. Add to a large serving bowl and top with cucumber, radishes, microgreens, and red pepper flakes. Serve warm or chilled.

Per Serving

Calories: 337 | Fat: 11.4 g | Protein: 13.3 g | Sodium: 760 mg
Fiber: 3.2 g | Carbohydrates: 50.9 g | Sugar: 1.6 g

Maple Baked Beans

Making your own baked beans is simple, and when you create your own at home, you're guaranteed to know exactly what's going into your food…and what you're leaving out of it! This puts you in the driver's seat and keeps your baked beans from turning into a sugar-laden, fattening food. Instead, you'll serve this tasty, protein-filled side dish with pride. And, while these Maple Baked Beans taste great right out of the bowl, you can also serve them with salad or even on some toast for breakfast.

Serves 4

Recipe Prep Time: *10 minutes*
Recipe Cook Time: *10 minutes*

1 tablespoon extra-virgin olive oil

½ cup peeled and finely chopped yellow onion

2 medium cloves garlic, peeled and minced

⅔ cup crushed tomatoes

2½ cups canned cannellini beans (rinsed and drained)

¼ cup pure maple syrup

1 tablespoon Dijon mustard

½ teaspoon paprika

⅛ teaspoon salt

¼ teaspoon black pepper

1 Heat oil in a medium sauté pan on medium-low. Add onions and cook 5–6 minutes until browned and softened, stirring occasionally.

2 Add garlic, tomatoes, beans, maple syrup, mustard, paprika, salt, and pepper. Reduce heat and simmer 5 minutes, stirring occasionally. Serve warm.

Per Serving

Calories: 246 | Fat: 3.8 g | Protein: 10.6 g | Sodium: 174 mg
Fiber: 8.4 g | Carbohydrates: 44.0 g | Sugar: 14.9 g

USE THE RIGHT MAPLE SYRUP

When buying maple syrup, it's important to look for pure maple syrup, not the kind that's mixed with sugar or corn syrup and used to pour over pancakes. You want it to be as clean as possible so you're not adding anything but extra sweetness to your dish.

CHAPTER 8

DINNER ENTRÉES

Barley Risotto with Peas and Asparagus

Traditional risotto is made with Arborio rice, but this recipe uses barley, which gives this risotto a lot more protein and fiber. This recipe uses quick-cook barley, so it will take you longer if you use the regular kind. In addition, this spring-inspired risotto is loaded with green vegetables, and although it is hearty, it will leave you feeling light and refreshed. If you're avoiding dairy, you can leave out the Parmesan cheese and the dish will still retain it's flavor, but you can always add some nutritional yeast for some faux cheesiness as well as extra protein.

Serves 4

Recipe Prep Time: *15 minutes*
Recipe Cook Time: *25 minutes*

½ pound (8 ounces) asparagus spears

2 tablespoons plus 1 teaspoon extra-virgin olive oil, divided

2½ cups low-sodium vegetable broth

½ medium yellow onion, peeled and chopped

2 large cloves garlic, peeled and finely chopped

1 large leek, thinly sliced (white part only)

1 cup quick-cook barley

Zest and juice of 2 small lemons

1½ cups English peas

½ cup grated Parmesan cheese

1 Preheat oven to 425°F. Drizzle asparagus with 1 teaspoon olive oil. Roast in the oven on a large baking pan 12–15 minutes. Chop asparagus into smaller pieces (about 1" long) to be added to the risotto.

2 While asparagus is roasting, bring broth to a boil in a small pan. Then lower the temperature just enough to keep warm.

3 In a large pot, heat remaining 2 tablespoons olive oil on medium. Add onion, garlic, and leek, and cook 5 minutes. Add barley and cook 1 minute, stirring occasionally.

4 Add lemon zest and ½ cup of the warm broth, and cook until broth is absorbed. Stir frequently. Continue adding broth in ½-cup increments until the barley is cooked and tender. When you have 1 cup left, add peas. Then continue to add the last cup ½ cup at a time.

5 Once all the broth has been added and absorbed, mix in the asparagus, lemon juice, and Parmesan cheese. Serve warm.

Per Serving

Calories: 367 | Fat: 9.7 g | Protein: 13.3 g | Sodium: 319 mg
Fiber: 13.1 g | Carbohydrates: 57.7 g | Sugar: 7.4 g

Spaghetti Squash Marinara with Lentil Meatballs

Everyone loves a good bowl of spaghetti and meatballs, and just because you're trying to eat a plant-based diet doesn't mean you can't enjoy the same dish—you just have to make some modifications. In this recipe, spaghetti squash is used instead of regular spaghetti, and lentils, mushrooms, and flaxseed are combined to create a protein-filled meatball with a texture that is surprisingly similar to the real deal.

Serves 2

Recipe Prep Time: *5 minutes*
Recipe Cook Time: *1 hour 45 minutes*

1 medium spaghetti squash
½ cup dried green lentils
1¼ cups water
1 tablespoon extra-virgin olive oil
½ small yellow onion, peeled and chopped
1 large clove garlic, peeled and finely chopped
½ cup chopped button mushrooms
½ tablespoon Dijon mustard
⅛ cup flaxseed meal
¼ teaspoon dried thyme
¼ teaspoon dried oregano
¼ teaspoon dried rosemary
¼ teaspoon paprika
¼ teaspoon ground nutmeg
½ teaspoon black pepper, divided
2 cups low-sodium marinara sauce
½ teaspoon dried parsley

1 Preheat oven to 400°F. Line a 10" × 15" baking sheet with aluminum foil. Cut squash in half lengthwise; scoop out and discard seeds and pulp.

2 Place squash cut-side down on the prepared baking sheet and bake 45–60 minutes or until easily pierced with a fork.

3 Meanwhile, add lentils and water to a medium saucepan and bring to a boil over medium-high heat. Reduce heat and simmer until tender and most of the liquid is absorbed, about 35–40 minutes.

4 While the lentils are cooking, heat olive oil in a large pan on medium-low. Add onion, garlic, and mushrooms and cook 5–7 minutes until mushrooms are soft and onions are translucent.

5 Add lentils to a medium bowl along with mustard, flaxseed, thyme, oregano, rosemary, paprika, nutmeg, and ¼ teaspoon pepper. Mix together, and then transfer to a blender or food processor. Blend on medium speed until mixture is a bit smoother but still has some texture, about 5–10 seconds. You don't want the meatballs to be too blended, so it's okay to have chunks of lentils, mushrooms, or onions in your sauce to give it a "meatier" texture.

6   When the squash is finished baking, scoop out the inside and add to a separate medium bowl; set aside. Lower oven temperature to 350°F. Line the baking sheet with new aluminum foil and spray with nonstick spray.

7   Form the lentil mixture into 2" balls and place them on the prepared baking sheet. Bake 35–45 minutes until meatballs firm up. They should be crisp on the outside but still a little soft on the inside.

8   Heat marinara in a large saucepan. Add spaghetti squash and mix until coated with sauce. Sprinkle with dried parsley and remaining black pepper. Top with meatballs, and serve warm.

Per Serving

Calories: 538 | Fat: 13.1 g | Protein: 21.1 g | Sodium: 186 mg
Fiber: 18.9 g | Carbohydrates: 87.5 g | Sugar: 28.3 g

SPAGHETTI SQUASH SUBSTITUTE

Using spaghetti squash makes this recipe nice and light, but if you don't have time to prepare it, you can use brown rice pasta instead. One benefit of making this change? You'll get a little extra protein.

Balsamic Tofu "Steaks" with Rosemary Potatoes and Mushrooms

Going plant-based can make people miss certain meals, and a way to solve this problem is to make meals, like this one, that "mimic" their meat-filled counterparts. This dish involves pan-searing tofu in the same style you would cook a steak, which results in a crispy outside and soft inside. The tofu is served with a side of mushrooms and potatoes, just like a steak dinner. If you want your tofu steak a bit richer, you can use a balsamic glaze instead of balsamic vinegar.

Serves 2

Recipe Prep Time: *30 minutes*
Recipe Cook Time: *20 minutes*

1 pound organic extra-firm tofu

1 cup sliced button mushrooms

1 medium russet potato, chopped

2 tablespoons extra-virgin olive oil, divided

1 teaspoon dried rosemary

¼ teaspoon salt

2 tablespoons balsamic vinegar, divided

¼ teaspoon black pepper

1. Place a paper towel on a plate and set tofu on top. Cover with another paper towel, and place a cutting board or another plate on top of the paper towel so it's pressing down on the tofu. Let sit 20 minutes. This will help drain the excess moisture from the tofu.

2. Preheat oven to 425°F. Line a 10" × 15" baking sheet with aluminum foil.

3. Toss together mushrooms, potatoes 1 tablespoon olive oil, rosemary, and salt in a medium bowl. Spread out evenly on the prepared baking sheet. Bake 20 minutes.

4. Cut tofu in half lengthwise and then again widthwise so you end up with 4 pieces. Heat the remaining 1 tablespoon olive oil in a large skillet on medium. Add tofu steaks, press down with a spatula, and cook 4 minutes on each side.

5. Pour 1 tablespoon balsamic vinegar over tofu and cook 1 minute. Flip, pour remaining 1 tablespoon balsamic vinegar over the other side, and cook 1 more minute. Serve warm alongside potatoes and mushrooms, and top everything with pepper.

Per Serving

Calories: 403 | Fat: 22.3 g | Protein: 25.9 g | Sodium: 318 mg
Fiber: 3.0 g | Carbohydrates: 28.2 g | Sugar: 4.9 g

Macro Bowl with Maple Turmeric Tahini Dressing

The idea of macrobiotic meals comes from traditional Eastern medicine, and these meals are all about balance and well-roundedness when it comes to the nutrients on your plate. Macro bowls usually include whole grains, pulses, vegetables, and fermented foods, with an emphasis on plant products. This recipe not only maintains that balance, but it also makes sure you get all the protein you need thanks to the brown rice, black beans, baby broccoli, and the tasty Maple Turmeric Tahini Dressing.

Serves 2

Recipe Prep Time: *15 minutes*
Recipe Cook Time: *20 minutes*

Macro Bowl

1 medium sweet potato, diced
1 bunch baby broccoli, stems removed
2 tablespoons extra-virgin olive oil
½ cup cooked brown rice
½ cup sauerkraut
½ large avocado, peeled and sliced
1 cup canned black beans (rinsed and drained)

Maple Turmeric Tahini Dressing

2 tablespoons tahini
2 teaspoons pure maple syrup
½ teaspoon turmeric powder
¼ teaspoon cayenne pepper

To Finish

¼ teaspoon pink Himalayan sea salt

1 **For Macro Bowl:** Preheat oven to 425°F. Line a 10" × 15" baking sheet with aluminum foil.

2 Spread sweet potato and baby broccoli on the prepared baking sheet. Drizzle olive oil over the top and bake 20 minutes.

3 Add brown rice to a serving bowl and top with sweet potato and broccoli mixture, sauerkraut, avocado, and black beans.

4 **For Maple Turmeric Tahini Dressing:** Combine dressing ingredients in a small bowl and whisk until smooth.

5 **To finish:** Top rice bowl with dressing and sea salt, and serve immediately.

Per Serving

Calories: 496 | Fat: 22.9 g | Protein: 14.2 g | Sodium: 535 mg
Fiber: 17.0 g | Carbohydrates: 60.0 g | Sugar: 8.6 g

Goat Cheese Ravioli

Most people don't have time to make pasta dough from scratch, but that doesn't mean you can't make your own ravioli at home. To make these, you only need to get fresh lasagna sheets, which you can find at the grocery store. If you can't find lasagna sheets, you can use wonton wrappers instead.

Makes 8 large ravioli

Recipe Prep Time: *20 minutes*
Recipe Cook Time: *3 minutes*

1 cup canned cannellini beans (rinsed and drained)

⅓ cup goat cheese

Juice of 2 small lemons, divided

3 tablespoons chopped fresh basil, divided

¼ teaspoon salt

4 fresh lasagna sheets

2 tablespoons crushed raw walnuts

1 tablespoon extra-virgin olive oil

¼ teaspoon black pepper

1 In a medium bowl, mash white beans with a fork until a paste forms. Mix in goat cheese, juice of 1 lemon, 2 tablespoons basil, and salt.

2 Take apart each lasagna sheet and run it under hot water for about 5 seconds on each side to soften. Lay on a flour-lined cutting board, and cut in half lengthwise using a pizza cutter.

3 Lay each half down vertically. Take 1 tablespoon of filling and put it in the center of the lasagna sheet, slightly toward the front. Fold over the lasagna sheet toward you, and press down the sides with a fork to seal filling inside. Use the pizza cutter to cut off any extra dough. The ravioli should be pretty large.

4 Bring a large pot of water to boil. Add ravioli and cook about 3 minutes until ravioli rise to the top. Drain and add to a bowl.

5 Top with walnuts, olive oil, remaining lemon juice, remaining 1 tablespoon basil, and pepper. Serve warm.

Per 1 ravioli

Calories: 100 | Fat: 4.0 g | Protein: 4.3 g | Sodium: 94 mg
Fiber: 1.9 g | Carbohydrates: 12.1 g | Sugar: 0.5 g

Rainbow Buddha Bowl

This beautiful dish is filled with vegetables in all the colors of the rainbow, but the healthy ingredients don't stop there. This recipe also uses chickpeas, hemp seeds, and chia seeds for protein, not to mention the Basil Lemon Tahini Sauce. This recipe packs in as many nutrients as possible. Some say this dish is called a Buddha Bowl because you stuff so much in, it's as round as a Buddha's belly.

Serves 2

Recipe Prep Time: *10 minutes*
Recipe Cook Time: *20 minutes*

Buddha Bowl

2 medium red beets

1 cup canned chickpeas (rinsed and drained)

1 tablespoon extra-virgin olive oil

¼ teaspoon black pepper

1 tablespoon coconut oil

4 cups fresh kale leaves

½ cup halved cherry tomatoes

½ large avocado, peeled and sliced

2 tablespoons hemp seeds

1 tablespoon chia seeds

Basil Lemon Tahini Sauce

2 tablespoons tahini

½ cup fresh basil leaves

Juice of 2 small lemons

½ tablespoon extra-virgin olive oil

1 tablespoon white wine vinegar

1 **For Buddha Bowl:** Preheat oven to 425°F. Line a 10" × 15" baking sheet with aluminum foil. Peel beets and cut into ½" slices crosswise.

2 Spread beets on the prepared baking sheet along with chickpeas. Drizzle olive oil over beets and chickpeas and top with black pepper. Bake 15–20 minutes until beets are soft and chickpeas are crispy.

3 Meanwhile, heat coconut oil on medium-low heat in a medium pan. Add kale and sauté 2 minutes or until leaves are soft.

4 Add kale to a serving bowl along with beets and chickpeas. Top with tomatoes, avocado, hemp seeds, and chia seeds.

5 **For Basil Lemon Tahini Sauce:** Add all sauce ingredients to a blender or food processor and blend on high speed until smooth, about 10–20 seconds. Pour over the mixture in the serving bowl, and serve immediately.

Per Serving

Calories: 540 | Fat: 35.2 g | Protein: 16.8 g | Sodium: 259 mg
Fiber: 15.4 g | Carbohydrates: 41.7 g | Sugar: 11.3 g

Mushroom Polenta Bowl with Greens and Beans

Polenta is a popular dish in Northern Italy, and because it's made from cornmeal, it contains some protein of its own. Polenta tends to thicken up quickly, so if you want it a bit thinner, just add a little bit of water or broth to loosen it up. And, if you make the cannellini beans yourself by cooking your own dried beans instead of using canned, you can overcook them a little so they get slightly crisp on the outside.

Serves 2

Recipe Prep Time: *15 minutes*
Recipe Cook Time: *15 minutes*

1½ cups water
⅛ teaspoon salt
½ cup polenta
1 tablespoon extra-virgin olive oil, divided
2 cups chopped rainbow chard
1 cup sliced cremini mushrooms
1 cup cooked or canned cannellini beans (rinsed and drained)
1 teaspoon ghee
¼ teaspoon black pepper

1. Bring water and salt to a boil in a medium pan. Stir in polenta, reduce heat to a simmer, and cover. Cook 10–15 minutes until all liquid is absorbed, stirring occasionally.

2. While polenta is cooking, heat ½ tablespoon olive oil in a large pan on medium-low. Add chard and cook 2–3 minutes or until wilted; set aside.

3. In the same pan, add another ½ tablespoon olive oil and keep on medium-low heat. Add mushrooms and cook 4–5 minutes until mushrooms have softened.

4. Add polenta to a serving bowl and top with chard, mushrooms, beans, and ghee (the ghee should melt into the bowl). Top with black pepper, and serve warm.

Per Serving

Calories: 318 | Fat: 10.4 g | Protein: 11.7 g | Sodium: 234 mg
Fiber: 8.8 g | Carbohydrates: 46.7 g | Sugar: 1.5 g

Pinto Burrito Bowl

Burritos aren't exactly considered health foods, but if you consider the beans and vegetables that are typically found inside a burrito, you may start to think of burritos in a different way. This version is prepared in a bowl with brown rice, so you don't get the refined carbohydrates from the tortilla. It's also completely vegan, which means no heavy sour cream or cheeses—although if you want to, you can add a dollop of Greek yogurt and a sprinkle of cheese at the end for extra flavor. And, if you like spicy, this bowl tastes especially good drizzled with hot sauce.

Serves 2

Recipe Prep Time: *15 minutes*
Recipe Cook Time: *30 minutes*

- 1 tablespoon extra-virgin olive oil
- 4 medium cloves garlic, peeled and minced
- ½ cup brown rice
- 1¼ cups low-sodium vegetable broth
- ½ cup no-salt-added diced tomatoes
- ½ teaspoon ground cumin
- ¼ teaspoon salt
- 2 tablespoons chopped fresh cilantro, divided
- 2 cups chopped romaine
- 1 (15-ounce) can pinto beans, rinsed and drained
- 1 cup cooked yellow corn kernels
- ½ cup chopped cherry tomatoes
- ½ large avocado, peeled and sliced
- Juice of 1 lime

1. Heat oil in a medium pot on medium-low. Add garlic and cook 1 minute. Add rice, broth, tomatoes, cumin, and salt. Bring to a boil, reduce to a simmer, and cover; cook about 30 minutes or until liquid is absorbed and rice is fluffy. When rice is finished cooking, stir in 1 tablespoon cilantro.

2. Add romaine to a serving bowl. Top with rice mixture, beans, corn, tomatoes, and avocado. Top off with lime juice and remaining cilantro, and serve warm.

Per Serving

Calories: 585 | Fat: 13.8 g | Protein: 19.5 g | Sodium: 737 mg
Fiber: 17.2 g | Carbohydrates: 99.5 g | Sugar: 9.0 g

WHERE TO FIND VEGAN CHEESE

If you don't eat dairy, you might be wondering where you can find some vegan cheese. Most major grocery stores carry Daiya, but Whole Foods is often a good source for nondairy cheese. I personally love Kite Hill's almond milk ricotta.

Harissa Tofu over Sesame Sweet Potato Noodles and Kale

So much of tofu's delicious taste comes from how you flavor it, and harissa, a North African chili-based paste, is full of flavor. For this recipe, you'll need a spiralizer to make the sweet potato noodles, but if you don't have one, you can just cut the sweet potato slices, drizzle some olive oil over them, and bake them for 20–25 minutes instead.

Serves 2

Recipe Prep Time: *15 minutes*
Recipe Cook Time: *15 minutes*

Harissa

2 tablespoons no-salt-added tomato paste
2 small cloves garlic, peeled and finely chopped
1 tablespoon chili powder
1 tablespoon ground cumin
½ teaspoon paprika
½ teaspoon ground caraway
1 tablespoon lemon juice
⅓ cup extra-virgin olive oil

Sweet Potato Noodles and Kale

1 large peeled sweet potato
1 tablespoon sesame oil
1 tablespoon extra-virgin olive oil
2 cups fresh kale leaves

Tofu

8 ounces organic extra-firm tofu
1 tablespoon chopped fresh Italian flat-leaf parsley

1. **For Harissa:** Prepare harissa by mixing ingredients together in a small bowl until smooth. Add 3 tablespoons harissa to a medium bowl (set the rest aside to save for another time).

2. **For Sweet Potato Noodles and Kale:** Cut off both ends of sweet potato and slice in half crosswise. Spiralize using a small noodle blade.

3. Heat sesame oil in a large pan on medium-low heat and add sweet potato noodles. Cover and cook 5–6 minutes until softened, stirring occasionally. Transfer to a large serving plate.

4. In a medium pan, heat olive oil on medium-low heat and add kale. Cook 3–4 minutes until wilted, stirring occasionally. Place kale on top of sweet potato noodles on serving plate.

5. **For Tofu:** Drain the tofu and pat dry with a paper towel. Slice tofu into ½" slices, and dip each side into the harissa so it's evenly coated. Heat the same pan the noodles were in on medium heat (no need to add more oil). Add tofu to the pan and cook each side 1–2 minutes until tofu begins to brown and crisp on the outside.

6. When tofu is ready, add to the plate with the sweet potato and kale, and top with any extra harissa if desired. Top with parsley, and serve warm.

Per Serving

Calories: 429 | Fat: 34.9 g | Protein: 13.6 g | Sodium: 99 mg
Fiber: 3.8 g | Carbohydrates: 17.7 g | Sugar: 4.2 g

Barbecue Tempeh Pizza

You may find yourself craving barbecue chicken pizza on your meat-free days (or just in general if you've given it up completely). Fortunately, this recipe gives you the flavors and tastes of the traditional version without packing your dish full of meat. Instead this dish uses tempeh, which has a crumbly and crispy texture that, once baked, resembles meat. This recipe makes a 12" pizza, which can be split between 3 lighter eaters or 2 very hungry ones.

Serves 2

Recipe Prep Time: *40 minutes*
Recipe Cook Time: *10 minutes*

- 1 pound whole-wheat pizza dough
- 8 ounces organic tempeh
- ¼ cup plus 2 tablespoons barbecue sauce, divided
- 1 cup shredded whole milk mozzarella cheese
- ¼ cup peeled and chopped white onion
- 1 tablespoon chopped fresh cilantro

1 Let dough rest on a floured surface for 30 minutes.

2 While dough is resting, crumble tempeh with your fingers and add to a medium bowl. Add ¼ cup barbecue sauce, and toss the tempeh until it's evenly coated.

3 Spread dough into a 12" circle, either stretching by hand or using a rolling pin. Lightly oil a baking sheet, pizza pan, or pizza stone, and add the dough.

4 Brush the top of the pizza dough with olive oil. Spread on the remaining 2 tablespoons barbecue sauce, leaving space for the crust on the edges. Top with cheese, tempeh, and onion. Bake 8–10 minutes or until cheese is bubbly and crust is golden. Remove from oven, top with cilantro, and serve warm.

Per Serving

Calories: 977 | Fat: 27.6 g | Protein: 49.3 g | Sodium: 1,813 mg
Fiber: 12.2 g | Carbohydrates: 126.0 g | Sugar: 19.0 g

Quinoa and Lentil Bowl with Golden Beets and Onion Jam

This Quinoa and Lentil Bowl requires a little bit of preparation and some multitasking, but once you taste the final result, you'll realize it's worth it. The rich onion jam and golden beets provide a slightly sweet flavor that's balanced out with the savory tang of the garlic tahini sauce. In this recipe the quinoa, lentils, and tahini sauce are loaded with protein, but the dish is also filled with fiber, so you really stay full.

Serves 2

Recipe Prep Time: *20 minutes*
Recipe Cook Time: *1 hour 15 minutes*

⅓ cup dried green lentils

2 cups water, divided

½ cup quinoa

2 medium golden beets

2 large cloves garlic (unpeeled)

2 tablespoons plus 1 teaspoon extra-virgin olive oil, divided

1 medium white onion, peeled and thinly sliced

2 tablespoons vegan Worcestershire sauce

3 tablespoons apple cider vinegar, divided

½ teaspoon coconut sugar

2 cups torn fresh kale leaves

2 tablespoons tahini

¼ cup lemon juice

⅛ teaspoon salt

⅛ teaspoon black pepper

1. Add lentils and 1 cup water to a medium pot and bring to a boil. Reduce heat and simmer until lentils are tender and most of the liquid is absorbed, about 35–40 minutes.

2. Meanwhile, add quinoa along with remaining 1 cup water to a medium saucepan and bring to a boil. Reduce to a simmer, cover, and cook until all the water is absorbed, about 10–15 minutes.

3. While the lentils and quinoa are cooking, preheat oven to 425°F. Line a 10" × 15" baking sheet with aluminum foil. Slice beets crosswise into ¼–½" slices and place on the prepared baking sheet. Trim off one end of the garlic cloves and place the unpeeled cloves on the baking sheet along with the beets. Drizzle both the beets and garlic with 1 tablespoon olive oil, and roast 25–30 minutes until beets are soft and crispy on the outside.

4. Heat 1 tablespoon olive oil in a large pan on medium-low heat; add onions and cook about 15 minutes until onions begin to brown, stirring occasionally. Add Worcestershire and 2 tablespoons vinegar, and cook 10 minutes. Add remaining

vinegar and sugar, and cook 5 more minutes until onions are soft and brown. Transfer onions to a small bowl and set aside.

5   Heat 1 teaspoon olive oil in the same pan on medium-low heat. Add kale and sauté 2–3 minutes until wilted. Remove from heat.

6   Add quinoa, lentils, and beets to a serving bowl. Add the onion jam to the bowl along with the kale.

7   Remove the skin from the roasted garlic. Prepare sauce by blending together garlic, tahini, lemon juice, salt, and pepper in a blender or food processor on high speed until smooth, about 10–20 seconds. Drizzle over bowl, and serve warm.

Per Serving

Calories: 555 | Fat: 22.6 g | Protein: 19.3 g | Sodium: 403 mg
Fiber: 11.7 g | Carbohydrates: 72.1 g | Sugar: 12.3 g

Edamame Pad Thai

Let's face it: as delicious as it is, pad thai isn't the healthiest of dinners. You also don't get much protein if you opt for a vegetarian version. However, with the few swaps made in this recipe, you can have a better-for-you meal with a balanced amount of nutrients. This colorful noodle dish is completely vegan, and the protein in this dinner comes from a combination of the brown rice noodles, edamame, sesame seeds, and the dash of peanut butter found in the sauce.

Serves 2

Recipe Prep Time: *20 minutes*
Recipe Cook Time: *5 minutes*

Pad Thai Sauce

2 tablespoons low-sodium soy sauce

1 tablespoon raw creamy peanut butter

1 tablespoon lime juice

1 tablespoon rice vinegar

½ tablespoon coconut sugar

¼ teaspoon red pepper flakes

Pad Thai

1 tablespoon sesame oil

1 medium red bell pepper, thinly sliced or spiralized

½ cup shredded carrots

1 cup cooked organic shelled edamame

4 ounces cooked brown rice pad thai noodles

To Finish

2 small green onions, finely chopped

3 sprigs fresh cilantro

1 teaspoon sesame seeds

1 **For Pad Thai Sauce:** Create sauce by mixing together ingredients in a small bowl until smooth.

2 **For Pad Thai:** In a large pan, heat sesame oil on medium. Add bell pepper and carrots, and cook 2–3 minutes.

3 Add edamame, noodles, and sauce to the pan and toss over low heat until well mixed and heated through, about 2 minutes.

4 **To finish:** Top with green onion, cilantro, and sesame seeds. Serve warm.

Per Serving

Calories: 513 | Fat: 19.6 g | Protein: 22.7 g | Sodium: 541 mg
Fiber: 12.0 g | Carbohydrates: 65.3 g | Sugar: 10.5 g

PAD THAI SWAPS

Feel like cutting down on carbs and adding in some veggies? Consider making this Edamame Pad Thai with spiralized zucchini or sweet potato instead of the noodles. You can also toss in some cubed tofu for extra protein.

Roasted Cauliflower and Chickpea Lemon Spaghetti with Arugula

This simple and light pasta dish is quick, but filled with flavor. It's both vegan and gluten-free, which makes it a friendly option for all diets. Using the brown rice spaghetti found in this dish is not only healthier, but it adds some additional protein to this entrée. And if you love leftovers, you're in luck. This meal practically begs you to save a little bit for lunch as it keeps well and even tastes good cold.

Serves 2

Recipe Prep Time: *20 minutes*
Recipe Cook Time: *25 minutes*

4 ounces uncooked brown rice spaghetti

2 cups lightly chopped cauliflower florets

1 (15-ounce) can chickpeas, rinsed and drained

2 tablespoons plus 1 teaspoon extra-virgin olive oil, divided

½ cup fresh arugula

Juice of 2 small lemons

¼ teaspoon black pepper

1 Preheat oven to 425°F. Line a large baking sheet with aluminum foil. Prepare pasta according to package instructions.

2 Spread cauliflower and chickpeas on the prepared baking sheet, keeping them separate. Drizzle 1 tablespoon olive oil on the cauliflower and 1 tablespoon olive oil on chickpeas. Toss chickpeas and cauliflower (separately) so everything is evenly coated. Bake about 20–25 minutes until cauliflower has begun to brown and chickpeas are crispy.

3 Place cooked pasta in a serving bowl. Add cauliflower, chickpeas, and arugula. Whisk together remaining 1 teaspoon olive and lemon juice in a small bowl and drizzle over spaghetti; toss the mixture until everything is evenly coated. Top with black pepper, and serve warm.

Per Serving

Calories: 499 | Fat: 15.8 g | Protein: 15.4 g | Sodium: 302 mg
Fiber: 14.5 g | Carbohydrates: 78.1 g | Sugar: 9.0 g

Coconut-Lime Tempeh Stir-Fry

A lot of people are afraid of tempeh because they don't know how to prepare it, but if you're not used to it, the best way to introduce it to your diet is to mix it in with other foods. In this citrusy dish, crumbled tempeh is mixed in with onions, mushrooms, red peppers, and spinach, and tossed with lime juice, soy sauce, and coconut. It's so flavorful and diverse, you'll forget you're even eating fermented soy.

Serves 2

Recipe Prep Time: *15 minutes*
Recipe Cook Time: *10 minutes*

1 tablespoon sesame oil
½ cup peeled and thinly sliced white onions
2 large cloves garlic, peeled and finely chopped
1 cup sliced button mushrooms
½ cup chopped red bell peppers
8 ounces organic tempeh, crumbled
2 cups fresh spinach leaves
Juice of 1 small lime
2 tablespoons low-sodium soy sauce
2 tablespoons unsweetened shredded coconut
¼ teaspoon red pepper flakes

1 Heat 1 tablespoon sesame oil in a large frying pan or wok on medium heat. Add onions, garlic, mushrooms, red peppers, and crumbled tempeh; sauté 5–7 minutes until onions are translucent and mushrooms soften.

2 Stir in spinach and lime and cook 1–2 minutes until spinach wilts. Mix in soy sauce, shredded coconut, and red pepper flakes; cook about 1 minute until heated through. Serve warm.

Per Serving

Calories: 358 | Fat: 20.4 g | Protein: 25.4 g | Sodium: 549 mg
Fiber: 2.9 g | Carbohydrates: 20.8 g | Sugar: 3.6 g

Hawaiian Tofu Poke Bowl

Poke bowls, which originate from Hawaii and consist of raw, cubed fish, have become trendy over the last few years. If you love the idea of a rice-based bowl with vegetables and beach-inspired flavors, this recipe allows you to make your own plant-based bowl using cubed tofu instead of fish. This poke bowl is prepared with many of the classics, including cucumber, edamame, and avocado, but it also adds the unique element of the Cara Cara oranges to give this dish a refreshing, tropical flavor.

Serves 2

Recipe Prep Time: *35 minutes*
Recipe Cook Time: *10 minutes*

½ cup uncooked brown rice

8 ounces organic extra-firm tofu

1 tablespoon sesame oil

1" knob gingerroot, peeled and minced

1 large clove garlic, peeled and minced

1 medium Persian cucumber, thinly sliced

½ cup cooked shelled edamame

½ Cara Cara orange, peeled and chopped

½ avocado, peeled and diced

1 large green onion, thinly sliced

2 teaspoons sesame seeds

2 tablespoons low-sodium soy sauce

Juice of 1 small lime

1   Prepare brown rice according to package instructions.

2   Pat tofu with a paper towel to soak up excess moisture. Cut into 1" cubes.

3   Heat sesame oil in a large pan on medium-low. Add ginger and garlic, and cook 1–2 minutes until fragrant. Add tofu and cook 6–7 minutes until tofu is golden brown. Be sure to turn the pieces over so they cook evenly on all sides. Remove tofu from heat and set aside. Let cool about 1 minute.

4   Add rice to a serving bowl. Top with tofu, sliced cucumber, edamame, orange, avocado, green onion, and sesame seeds. Top with soy sauce and lime juice, and serve immediately.

Per Serving

Calories: 523 | Fat: 23.6 g | Protein: 25.6 g | Sodium: 526 mg
Fiber: 9.2 g | Carbohydrates: 55.2 g | Sugar: 6.8 g

"Chorizo" Rice Bowl

Typically, chorizo is a Spanish pork sausage made with smoked paprika and other spices, but this plant-based version is made with tofu instead. Although it's not an exact replica of traditional chorizo, this vegan copycat has a similar texture and flavor and can be served the same way as regular chorizo. This "Chorizo" Rice Bowl is so delicious that you won't even miss the meat!

Serves 4

Recipe Prep Time: *5 minutes*
Recipe Cook Time: *50 minutes*

Rice and Potato

1 cup uncooked brown rice
2½ cups low-sodium vegetables broth
½ cup no-salt-added diced tomatoes
½ teaspoon salt
1 large sweet potato, diced
1 tablespoon extra-virgin olive oil

Chorizo

8 ounces organic firm tofu
¼ cup finely chopped oil-packed sun-dried tomatoes
⅓ cup finely chopped button mushrooms
4 small cloves garlic, peeled and minced
¼ cup peeled and minced white onion
2 tablespoons apple cider vinegar
1½ tablespoons chili powder
½ teaspoon cayenne pepper
¾ teaspoon paprika
½ teaspoon ground cumin
⅛ teaspoon salt
¼ teaspoon black pepper
1 tablespoon extra-virgin olive oil

To Finish

1 medium avocado, peeled and sliced

1 **For Rice:** Add rice, broth, tomatoes, and salt to a medium pot, and bring to a boil. Reduce to a simmer, cover, and cook 30 minutes or until broth is absorbed.

2 **For Potato:** Preheat oven to 425°F. Line a 10" × 15" baking sheet with aluminum foil. Spread sweet potatoes evenly on the baking sheet and drizzle with olive oil. Bake 20 minutes or until potatoes just begin to crisp on the outside.

3 **For Chorizo:** Drain tofu and pat it dry with a paper towel. Add to a large bowl and mash with a fork until crumbled. Add sun-dried tomatoes, mushrooms, garlic, white onion, apple cider vinegar, chili powder, cayenne pepper, paprika, cumin, salt, and pepper. Toss until the mixture is evenly coated with the spices.

4 Heat oil in a large frying pan on medium. Add chorizo mixture and cook 6–7 minutes, stirring occasionally, until slightly crispy.

5 **To finish:** Add rice to bowls, and top with sweet potato, chorizo, and avocado. Serve warm.

Per Serving

Calories: 380 | Fat: 13.6 g | Protein: 12.0 g | Sodium: 508 mg
Fiber: 7.6 g | Carbohydrates: 54.1 g | Sugar: 3.6 g

Coconut Turmeric Chickpeas with Quinoa and Mint Yogurt Sauce

This Indian-inspired dinner might sound fancy, but it's the perfect meal to make when you don't feel like whipping out a ton of ingredients—or taking up a ton of time. Here, chickpeas are simmered in a a simple sauce of coconut milk and turmeric and are served over a bed of quinoa and arugula with a dollop of Mint Yogurt Sauce—you can have dinner on your table in 30 minutes flat!

Serves 4

Recipe Prep Time: *15 minutes*
Recipe Cook Time: *18 minutes*

Mint Yogurt Sauce

1 cup 2% plain Greek yogurt
⅓ cup fresh mint leaves
Juice of 2 small lemons
1 tablespoon extra-virgin
   olive oil

Chickpeas and Quinoa

1 cup uncooked quinoa
2 cups water
1 cup canned coconut milk
1 (15-ounce) can chickpeas,
   rinsed and drained
1 teaspoon turmeric powder
½ teaspoon dried oregano
1 tablespoon chopped fresh
   Italian flat-leaf parsley
2 cups fresh arugula

1 **For Mint Yogurt Sauce:** Add all ingredients to a blender or food processor and blend on high speed until mint is processed and smooth, about 20–30 seconds.

2 **For Chickpeas and Quinoa:** Add quinoa and water to a medium saucepan and bring to a boil over medium-high heat. Reduce to a simmer, cover, and cook until all the water is absorbed, about 10–15 minutes.

3 In a large pan, heat coconut milk on medium heat until it just begins to boil. Lower to medium-low and add chickpeas, turmeric, oregano, and parsley. Simmer 2–3 minutes to let the flavors set.

4 Add quinoa to a serving bowl along with arugula. Add coconut chickpeas and top with a dollop of yogurt sauce. Serve warm.

Per Serving

Calories: 436 | Fat: 19.3 g | Protein: 17.8 g | Sodium: 165 mg
Fiber: 7.6 g | Carbohydrates: 47.9 g | Sugar: 5.5 g

CHAPTER 9

CASSEROLES AND BAKES

Vegetable Polenta Bake

Polenta's creamy texture makes it perfect for the inside of a gooey bake. And, because polenta is made of corn, it provides some additional protein along with the kidney beans. Throw on some peppers, onions, tomatoes, artichokes, kidney beans, and just a little bit of Parmesan cheese, and you have an easy meal that appeals to both gourmands and picky eaters alike.

Serves 8

Recipe Prep Time: *30 minutes*
Recipe Cook Time: *25 minutes*

- 2 cups uncooked polenta
- 1½ tablespoons extra-virgin olive oil, divided
- 1 medium yellow onion, peeled and sliced
- 1 large red bell pepper
- 1 medium yellow bell pepper
- 2 (15-ounce) cans kidney beans, rinsed and drained
- 1 cup chopped artichoke hearts
- ½ cup halved cherry tomatoes, halved
- ¼ cup grated Parmesan cheese
- ½ tablespoons bread crumbs

1 Preheat oven to 375°F. Lightly grease a 9" × 13" baking dish with cooking spray. Cook polenta according to package instructions.

2 In a large pan, heat 1 tablespoon olive oil on medium-low. Add onions and bell peppers and cook 4–5 minutes until onions are translucent. Mix in kidney beans and remove from heat.

3 Spread polenta evenly on the bottom of the prepared baking dish. Spread the onion, pepper, and bean mixture over the polenta. Top with artichokes and tomatoes, and drizzle on the remaining ½ tablespoon olive oil. Finish off with Parmesan and bread crumbs, and bake 20 minutes or until cheese begins to bubble. Serve immediately.

Per Serving

Calories: 256 | Fat: 4.7 g | Protein: 10.2 g | Sodium: 280 mg
Fiber: 9.9 g | Carbohydrates: 44.3 g | Sugar: 1.6 g

Moroccan Chickpea Skillet Bake

Bask in the flavors of Morocco with this vegan Moroccan Chickpea Skillet Bake. In this protein-packed dish, chickpeas and eggplant are baked in tomato sauce flavored with Moroccan spices and topped off with bread crumbs and parsley. And, since everyone hates cleaning the kitchen, everything is made in one pan, so you won't have to worry about using too many dishes.

Serves 4

Recipe Prep Time: *10 minutes*
Recipe Cook Time: *28 minutes*

2 tablespoons extra-virgin olive oil, divided.

4 medium cloves garlic, peeled and finely chopped

1 medium yellow onion, peeled and chopped

1 (14-ounce) can no-salt-added diced tomatoes

¼ cup no-salt-added tomato paste

1 tablespoon chili powder

1 tablespoon ground cumin

1 teaspoon paprika

1 tablespoon lemon juice

2 cups chopped purple globe eggplant (unpeeled)

1 (15-ounce) can chickpeas, rinsed and drained

2 tablespoons bread crumbs

1 tablespoon finely chopped fresh Italian flat-leaf parsley

1 Preheat oven to 450°F. Heat oil in a large cast-iron skillet or oven-safe pan on medium-low. Add garlic and cook 1 minute. Add onions and cook 3–4 minutes until onions begin to soften. Add diced tomatoes, tomato paste, chili powder, cumin, paprika, and lemon juice; mix together and simmer 2–3 minutes.

2 Mix in eggplant and chickpeas, making sure they're completely covered by tomato mixture. Cover with bread crumbs. Drizzle remaining 1 tablespoon olive oil over bread crumbs. Transfer skillet to the oven and bake 20 minutes.

3 Remove from oven and let cool 10–15 minutes. Top with parsley, and serve warm.

___

Per Serving

Calories: 231 | Fat: 8.5 g | Protein: 8.0 g | Sodium: 295 mg
Fiber: 9.2 g | Carbohydrates: 32.9 g | Sugar: 10.8 g

Black Bean Enchilada Bake

Most people stick to eating enchiladas at Mexican restaurants, but they're pretty easy to make at home, especially if you make them more like a casserole. This Black Bean Enchilada Bake doesn't use meat or chicken, but it is loaded with black beans, spinach, and red bell peppers—and a quick and easy enchilada sauce that's guaranteed to wake up your taste buds. However, if you don't feel like taking the time to make the sauce, you can always skip this step and purchase some ready-made enchilada sauce at the store.

Serves 6

Recipe Prep Time: *20 minutes*
Recipe Cook Time: *50 minutes*

Enchilada Sauce
1 tablespoon extra-virgin olive oil
1 tablespoon whole-wheat flour
3½ teaspoons chili powder
½ teaspoon ground cumin
¼ teaspoon garlic powder
¼ teaspoon dried oregano
½ teaspoon cayenne pepper
1 cup no-sugar-added tomato sauce
1 cup low-sodium vegetable broth

Enchiladas
12 (6") corn tortillas
2 (15-ounce) cans black beans, rinsed and drained
1 medium red bell pepper, seeded and finely chopped
1 cup fresh spinach leaves
½ cup shredded Mexican blend cheese
2 small green onions, finely chopped
1 medium avocado, peeled and sliced

1 Preheat oven to 375°F.

2 **For Enchilada Sauce:** In a medium saucepan, heat olive oil on medium heat. Add flour and stir until flour is evenly coated with oil. Add chili powder, cumin, garlic powder, oregano, and cayenne pepper until mixed evenly. Add tomato sauce and vegetable broth. Stir and bring to a boil. Reduce heat and simmer 10 minutes, stirring occasionally.

3 **For Enchiladas:** Grease a 7" × 13" baking dish with cooking spray. Layer 6 corn tortillas on the bottom of the pan. In a large bowl, combine black beans, red bell peppers, and half of the enchilada sauce. Spread evenly over tortillas in the baking dish. Spread spinach on top of that evenly. Layer on 6 more corn tortillas. Top with remaining enchilada sauce and spread so the tortillas are covered.

4 Transfer to the oven and bake 20 minutes. Remove from oven, sprinkle with cheese, and return to the oven. Bake another 15–20 minutes until cheese just begins to get crispy. Let cool 5–10 minutes. Top with green onion and avocado and serve warm.

Per Serving

Calories: 356 | Fat: 9.4 g | Protein: 15.0 g | Sodium: 444 mg
Fiber: 15.6 g | Carbohydrates: 54.2 g | Sugar: 2.5 g

White Bean Ratatouille Casserole

Although the word *ratatouille* might sound too gourmet to create in your home kitchen, this stewed vegetable dish actually isn't too difficult to make. The vegetables and flavors of a traditional ratatouille from the Provence region of France inspired this recipe, but this dish is baked into a casserole with a white bean purée, which makes it more of a complete meal.

Serves 6

Recipe Prep Time: *25 minutes*
Recipe Cook Time: *1 hour*

1½ cups canned no-salt-added diced tomatoes

½ cup no-salt-added tomato paste

2 tablespoons extra-virgin olive oil, divided

2 large cloves garlic, peeled and minced

1 tablespoon fresh sliced basil

½ teaspoon dried oregano

2 (15-ounce) cans cannellini beans, rinsed and drained

½ large eggplant, thinly sliced

1 medium zucchini, thinly sliced

1 medium yellow squash, thinly sliced

2 medium tomatoes, thinly sliced

¼ teaspoon salt

¼ teaspoon black pepper

1 Preheat oven to 350°F. Grease a 10" × 6" baking dish with cooking spray. In a medium bowl, combine diced tomatoes, tomato paste, 1 tablespoon olive oil, garlic, basil, and oregano. Spread on the bottom of the baking dish evenly using a spatula.

2 Make bean paste by either mashing white beans with a fork or puréeing in a food processor or blender on high until smooth, about 10–20 seconds. Spread the white bean purée over the tomato sauce layer.

3 Top white bean layer with rows of alternating veggies. Lay down a slice of eggplant, followed by a zucchini slice, then a slice of yellow squash, and then a tomato slice, until it makes a complete row. Repeat until the entire white bean layer is covered. Then make another row of vegetables on top of the first. Top with remaining 1 tablespoon olive oil, salt, and pepper, and bake about 1 hour. Let cool slightly before serving.

Per Serving

Calories: 222 | Fat: 5.0 g | Protein: 11.7 g | Sodium: 139 mg
Fiber: 10.4 g | Carbohydrates: 35.6 g | Sugar: 7.9 g

Lentil Meatloaf

This Lentil Meatloaf is hearty, filling, and free of beef, but it can help satisfy that craving when you're in the mood for comfort food. It's already pretty moist as is, but you can prepare extra glaze if you like your meatloaf a bit saucier.

Serves 6

Recipe Prep Time: *20 minutes*
Recipe Cook Time: *90 minutes*

Tomato Glaze

¼ cup no-salt-added tomato paste

½ tablespoon Dijon mustard

1 tablespoon apple cider vinegar

1 tablespoon raw wild honey

1 tablespoon low-sodium soy sauce

Meatloaf

1 cup dried green lentils

2½ cups water

1 tablespoon extra-virgin olive oil

½ medium yellow onion, peeled and chopped

½ cup chopped carrots

3 cups sliced button mushrooms

2 large cloves garlic

¼ cup no-salt-added tomato paste

3 tablespoons low-sodium soy sauce

½ teaspoon dried thyme

½ teaspoon dried oregano

1½ cups rolled oats

Per Serving

Calories: 259 | Fat: 4.2 g | Protein: 13.6 g
Sodium: 372 mg | Fiber: 7.3 g
Carbohydrates: 44.7 g | Sugar: 8.3 g

1. Preheat oven to 375°F.

2. **For Tomato Glaze:** Combine all glaze ingredients in a small bowl and mix until smooth.

3. **For Meatloaf:** First, prepare lentils. Add lentils and water to a medium saucepan and bring to a boil. Reduce heat and simmer until lentils are tender and most of the liquid is absorbed, about 35–40 minutes.

4. While lentils are cooking, heat olive oil in a large skillet on medium. Add onions and carrots, and cook 5 minutes, stirring occasionally. Add mushrooms and garlic, and cook 6–7 minutes more or until vegetables are soft. Stir occasionally.

5. Add half of the lentils and the vegetable mixture to a blender or food processor along with tomato paste, soy sauce, thyme, and oregano. Pulse together until ingredients are combined, but not too blended, about 5–10 seconds. You want the mixture to have a chunky texture similar to ground meat.

6. In a large mixing bowl, combine lentil mixture, remaining plain lentils, and oats. Line a 10" × 15" baking sheet with aluminum foil. Dump the mixture onto the baking sheet and form it into a loaf. It should be about 8" × 4".

7. Spread half of the glaze over the top and on the sides. Bake 30 minutes. Remove from oven and spread on the rest of the glaze; return to the oven and bake another 10 minutes. Slice to serve.

Tofu "Ricotta" Veggie Lasagna

Lasagna typically doesn't have much protein in it unless you add meat, but this lasagna is sneaky. Instead of using regular ricotta as a filling, tofu ricotta is used instead, and it tastes strikingly similar when baked between all those layers. In addition, spinach and zucchini add some vegetables to the lasagna, and a layer of mozzarella is baked on top for some crisp cheesiness. If you're vegan, skip this step. The rest of the lasagna is completely plant-based, and the top layer of cheese won't affect the taste all that much.

Serves 6

Recipe Prep Time: *30 minutes*
Recipe Cook Time: *40 minutes*

Tofu "Ricotta"

15½ ounces organic firm tofu
3 tablespoons nutritional yeast
2 tablespoons lemon juice
3 tablespoons filtered water
½ teaspoon garlic powder
¼ teaspoon salt
¼ teaspoon black pepper
⅓ cup fresh basil leaves

Lasagna

1 pound no-boil lasagna noodles
2 tablespoons extra-virgin olive oil
1 pound frozen spinach
2 medium green zucchinis, chopped
1 medium yellow onion, peeled and chopped
2 cups marinara sauce
1 cup shredded mozzarella cheese

1 Preheat oven to 350°F.

2 **For Tofu "Ricotta":** Squeeze out any excess water from the tofu using paper towels. Add tofu and remaining ingredients to a food processor or blender and pulse until just smooth. You don't want to blend too much or the ricotta will become more of a purée. Set aside.

3 **For Lasagna:** Prepare lasagna noodles according to package directions. Skip this step if you are using no-boil noodles. Set aside.

4 In a large pan, heat olive oil on medium-low heat. Add spinach, zucchini, and onions, and cook 6–8 minutes until vegetables have softened.

5 Grease a 9" × 13" baking dish with cooking spray. Line the bottom with a single layer of lasagna noodles. Top with a layer of ricotta (about ⅓ of the ricotta), followed by a layer of marinara (½ cup), followed by a layer of the spinach and zucchini (about ⅓).

6 Add another layer of noodles, and repeat with all the layers until you have 3 of each. Finish off with a remaining layer of noodles, marinara, and mozzarella cheese. Bake 30–40 minutes. Broil on high 2 minutes to crisp the top layer. Let cool slightly before serving.

Per Serving

Calories: 492 | Fat: 15.5 g | Protein: 26.7 g | Sodium: 344 mg
Fiber: 7.8 g | Carbohydrates: 60.4 g | Sugar: 8.1 g

Tomato Lima Bean Bake

Lima beans are a great source of protein, but unfortunately, many people don't like the idea of these beans, as lima beans tend to get a bad rap as being gross or unpalatable. If you're one of those people, give this Mediterranean-inspired bake a try—it might change your mind about the bean. This recipe uses dried lima beans to start, and you can use regular lima beans or heirloom lima beans—also known as Christmas lima beans thanks to their speckled color—which tend to have a creamier, more potato-like flavor than regular lima beans.

Serves 4

Recipe Prep Time: *20 minutes*
Recipe Cook Time: *65 minutes*

- 1 cup dried lima beans, soaked in water overnight
- 1 bay leaf
- 1 tablespoon plus 1 teaspoon extra-virgin olive oil, divided
- 4 medium cloves garlic, peeled and finely chopped
- ½ medium white onion, peeled and chopped
- 3 cups crushed tomatoes
- ½ teaspoon dried thyme
- ½ teaspoon dried oregano
- ¼ teaspoon salt
- ¼ teaspoon black pepper
- 3 tablespoons crumbled feta cheese
- 2 tablespoons chopped fresh Italian flat-leaf parsley

1 Drain beans and add to a large pot. Cover completely with water. Add bay leaf and bring to a boil. Reduce to a simmer, cover, and cook 35–45 minutes until beans soften but still hold their shape.

2 Meanwhile, preheat oven to 400°F. Heat 1 tablespoon oil in a large skillet on medium-low. Add garlic and onions, and cook 4–5 minutes until onions are soft and translucent. Add crushed tomatoes, thyme, oregano, salt, and pepper. Increase heat to medium and cook until sauce comes to a boil. Reduce to a simmer, cover, and cook 15–20 minutes until sauce thickens. Stir occasionally.

3 Add the beans to the sauce (draining any leftover liquid from the beans if necessary) and toss to coat.

4 Transfer the contents of the skillet into a large oval gratin dish or 9" square or round baking dish. Top with feta and bake 20 minutes. Let cool slightly. Top with parsley and drizzle with remaining 1 teaspoon olive oil. Serve warm.

Per Serving

Calories: 169 | Fat: 6.4 g | Protein: 7.0 g | Sodium: 550 mg
Fiber: 5.8 g | Carbohydrates: 23.8 g | Sugar: 9.4 g

WHY YOU SHOULD TRY CHRISTMAS LIMA BEANS

Lima beans get a bad rap, but not only do heirloom lima beans look more appetizing (they're larger and are white and brown in color), but they tend to taste better, similar almost to a chestnut.

Lentil Moussaka

Moussaka is a Middle Eastern dish that is typically made with eggplant, potato, and ground meat. This spin on Greek-style moussaka is filled with eggplant, and lentils are used instead of ground meat for protein. To make the dish healthier, a combination of Greek yogurt and Parmesan cheese is used instead of béchamel sauce, but it still provides that crispy, cheesy outer layer that makes Greek moussaka so delicious.

Serves 6

Recipe Prep Time: *20 minutes*
Recipe Cook Time: *1 hour 25 minutes*

¾ cup dried green lentils
2 cups water
1 large eggplant
3 tablespoons extra-virgin olive oil, divided
1 medium yellow onion, peeled and diced
3 large cloves garlic, peeled and finely chopped
2 tablespoons no-salt-added tomato paste
1 (15-ounce) can no-salt-added diced tomatoes
¼ teaspoon ground cinnamon
¼ teaspoon dried oregano
¼ teaspoon salt
¼ teaspoon black pepper
1 cup plain 2% Greek yogurt
½ cup grated Parmesan cheese
¼ teaspoon ground nutmeg

1 Preheat oven to 350°F. Grease a 7" × 13" baking dish with cooking spray.

2 Add lentils and water to a medium pot and bring to a boil. Reduce to a simmer, cover, and cook 45 minutes or until lentils are soft and water is absorbed.

3 While lentils are cooking, slice eggplant into ¼" rounds and then cut rounds into quarters. Heat 2 tablespoons olive oil in a large pan on medium heat. Add eggplant and cook 7–10 minutes until eggplant has softened. Remove from pan and set aside.

4 Add remaining 1 tablespoon oil to the pan and reduce heat to medium-low. Add onions and garlic; cook 4–5 minutes until onions have softened. Add tomato paste, diced tomatoes, cinnamon, oregano, salt, and pepper; simmer 4–5 minutes.

5 Add lentils and eggplant to the mixture and stir to combine. Transfer to prepared baking dish.

6 In a medium bowl, combine yogurt, Parmesan, and nutmeg, Spoon mixture on top of vegetable mixture and bake 30–40 minutes until top is slightly golden brown. Serve warm.

Per Serving

Calories: 253 | Fat: 9.7 g | Protein: 13.9 g | Sodium: 293 mg
Fiber: 6.6 g | Carbohydrates: 28.9 g | Sugar: 8.2 g

Green Chili Rice and Bean Casserole

Rice and beans together make a great protein, and this Mexican-inspired casserole is flavorful way to enjoy the combo. You can eat it by itself, but you can also use the leftovers in tacos, burritos, or even in a salad. Feel free to top it off with sliced green onion and avocado, if desired.

Serves 8

Recipe Prep Time: *10 minutes*
Recipe Cook Time: *40 minutes*

- 1 tablespoon extra-virgin olive oil
- 1 large yellow onion, peeled and chopped
- 1 medium red bell pepper, seeded and chopped
- 2 medium cloves garlic, peeled and finely chopped
- 1 (7-ounce) can diced mild green chilies
- 1 (15-ounce) can black beans, rinsed and drained
- 1 (15-ounce) can kidney beans, rinsed and drained
- 2 cups cooked brown rice
- ¼ cup low-sodium vegetable broth
- 1 tablespoon chili powder
- 1 teaspoon ground cumin
- 1 cup shredded sharp Cheddar cheese

1 Heat oil in a large pan on medium. Add onions and bell pepper, and cook 4–5 minutes until onions are translucent.

2 Add onions and peppers to a large bowl, along with garlic, green chilies, black beans, kidney beans, brown rice, vegetable broth, chili powder, and cumin.

3 Transfer to a 7" × 11.5" baking dish, and top with cheese. Bake 25–35 minutes until cheese is bubbling. Let cool slightly before serving.

Per Serving

Calories: 235 | Fat: 6.7 g | Protein: 11.2 g | Sodium: 368 mg
Fiber: 8.4 g | Carbohydrates: 31.8 g | Sugar: 1.4 g

Lemon Chickpea Bake

It's hard to make a bake that doesn't require any eggs or cheese as a binder, but this lemony chickpea bake is completely vegan. In this delicious dish, tahini holds the bake together, which not only adds some flavor, but some protein as well. And, in addition to being incredibly flavorful and full of plant-based proteins, this dish is made in one pan, which makes cleanup a breeze. Also, if you're looking to impress your guests, top this dish with a few basil leaves and a lemon slice to make it look as fancy as it tastes!

Serves 6

Recipe Prep Time: *15 minutes*
Recipe Cook Time: *40 minutes*

- 1 tablespoon extra-virgin olive oil
- ½ large onion, peeled and diced
- 1 large russet potato, diced
- 2 large cloves garlic, peeled and finely chopped
- 2 (15-ounce) cans chickpeas, rinsed and drained
- ½ cup tahini
- Juice and zest of 1 large lemon
- 1 tablespoon bread crumbs
- ¼ teaspoon salt
- 4 fresh basil leaves, chopped

1 Preheat oven to 375°F.

2 Heat olive oil in a large oven-safe skillet on medium-low. Add onions and potatoes, and cook 6–8 minutes until onions are translucent and potatoes begin to soften.

3 Remove from heat and mix in chickpeas, tahini, lemon juice and zest, bread crumbs, salt, and pepper until well combined. Transfer to the oven and bake 30 minutes. Remove from oven and let cool slightly. Top with basil, and serve.

Per Serving

Calories: 311 | Fat: 14.0 g | Protein: 11.0 g | Sodium: 319 mg
Fiber: 8.3 g | Carbohydrates: 36.4 g | Sugar: 4.6 g

Curry Lentil and Wild Rice Casserole

This vegan and gluten-free casserole is as loaded with plant- proteins as it is with spices. Here, lentils, wild rice, and sweet potatoes are cooked in a curry coconut sauce laden with Indian-inspired flavors.

Serves 8

Recipe Prep Time: 25 minutes
Recipe Cook Time: 1 hour 30 minutes

5½ cups water, divided
1 cup wild rice
1 cup dried green lentils
2 tablespoons extra-virgin olive oil
2 large cloves garlic, peeled and finely chopped
1 large yellow onion, peeled and diced
1 large sweet potato, cut into small cubes
1 cup canned coconut milk
½ teaspoon curry powder
½ teaspoon ground cumin
¼ teaspoon ground cardamom
¼ cup nutritional yeast
2 tablespoons unsweetened shredded coconut

1 Preheat oven to 350°F. Grease a 7" × 13" baking dish with cooking spray. In a medium pot, prepare wild rice. Bring 3 cups water to a boil. Add rice, reduce to a simmer, and cover. Cook 45–50 minutes until rice softens but is still a bit firm.

2 Meanwhile, in a separate medium pot, cook lentils. Add lentils and 2½ cups water to a medium saucepan, and bring to a boil. Reduce heat and simmer until lentils are tender and the liquid is almost all the way absorbed, about 35–40 minutes.

3 In a large pan, heat oil on medium heat. Add garlic, onions, and sweet potato, and cook 7–8 minutes until onions are translucent and sweet potato softens a little. Cover if necessary to help get potatoes cooking.

4 When wild rice and lentils are ready, add to the pan and mix everything together. In a small pot, heat coconut milk and mix in curry powder, cumin, and cardamom. Cook 1–2 minutes on medium-low heat, stirring until the spices mix into the coconut milk.

5 Pour the curry coconut milk into the pan with the casserole mixture, and mix until everything is evenly coated. Transfer to the baking dish. Sprinkle nutritional yeast and coconut on top, and bake 30 minutes.

Per Serving
Calories: 279 | Fat: 10.3 g | Protein: 11.1 g | Sodium: 19 mg
Fiber: 5.2 g | Carbohydrates: 37.2 g | Sugar: 2.5 g

Southwestern Spaghetti Squash Casserole

This Tex–Mex-inspired casserole is perfect to make when you have leftover spaghetti squash or you're looking for a meal that's lower in carbs. Here black beans provide protein, and the green bell peppers, corn, and jalapeño give this bake its Southwestern flavors.

Serves 8

Recipe Prep Time: *50 minutes*
Recipe Cook Time: *1 hour 20 minutes*

2 medium spaghetti squash

1 tablespoon extra-virgin olive oil

1 medium yellow onion, peeled and chopped

1 medium green bell pepper, chopped

1 medium jalapeño, chopped and seeds removed

2 large cloves garlic, peeled and finely chopped

2 (15-ounce) cans black beans

1 cup frozen organic yellow corn, thawed

1 teaspoon ground cumin

1 tablespoon chili powder

1½ cups grated sharp Cheddar cheese

1 Preheat oven to 375°F, and grease a 9" × 13" baking dish with cooking spray. Cut spaghetti squash in half lengthwise; remove and discard pulp and seeds. Place cut-side down on a large baking sheet and bake 45–50 minutes until easily pierced with a fork. Lower oven temperature to 350°F.

2 While spaghetti squash is cooking, heat oil in a large pan on medium. Add onions, peppers, jalapeño, and garlic, and cook 4–5 minutes until peppers and onions soften.

3 Remove from heat, and add to a large bowl. Scoop out the spaghetti squash, and squeeze out some of the excess water using your hands or by soaking it up with a paper towel. This will help prevent the casserole from getting watery.

4 Add spaghetti squash to the bowl along with black beans, corn, cumin, chili powder, and ½ cup cheese. Mix together until everything is evenly coated. If it doesn't fit in the bowl, you can add it to the casserole dish and mix it in there.

5 Transfer the contents of the bowl to the baking dish, spreading evenly. Sprinkle the remaining Cheddar on top and bake 25–30 minutes until cheese has melted on top and is beginning to get crispy.

Per Serving

Calories: 280 | Fat: 8.8 g | Protein: 13.8 g | Sodium: 346 mg
Fiber: 11.4 g | Carbohydrates: 37.6 g | Sugar: 6.9 g

Pasta Bake

There is nothing like the comfort of warm, cheesy pasta when you're having a bad day, when it's cold outside, or when you're just craving something that will make your taste buds happy. But this Pasta Bake provides more than just comfort: it's filled with protein, fiber, and other nutrients to help you power through even the roughest of days. Make sure you use brown rice pasta in this bake. It's not only healthier than white pasta, but it provides more protein.

Serves 8

Recipe Prep Time: *30 minutes*
Recipe Cook Time: *1 hour*

- 1 (28-ounce) can whole peeled San Marzano tomatoes
- 3 tablespoons no-salt-added tomato paste
- 1 pound thawed frozen spinach (squeeze out excess liquid)
- ¼ cup hemp seeds
- ¼ cup chia seeds
- 2 large cloves garlic, peeled and minced
- 1 teaspoon dried basil
- 1 teaspoon dried oregano
- 1 teaspoon dried thyme
- ¼ teaspoon salt
- ½ teaspoon black pepper
- ¼ teaspoon red pepper flakes
- 1 cup low-sodium vegetable broth
- 1½ cups water
- 1 pound brown rice penne pasta
- 1 cup ricotta cheese
- ½ cup grated Parmesan cheese

1 Preheat oven to 375°F. Grease a 9" × 13" baking dish with cooking spray.

2 Crush whole tomatoes and add to the prepared dish. Add tomato paste, thawed spinach, hemp seeds, chia seeds, garlic, dried herbs, vegetable broth, and water. Stir until evenly combined.

3 Add pasta and ricotta, and stir again so that the pasta is evenly coated and submerged in the sauce. Top with Parmesan and cover. Bake 45 minutes, then uncover and bake an additional 15 minutes. Broil 1–2 minutes on high if you want the cheese on top to be crispy.

Per Serving

Calories: 381 | Fat: 12.5 g | Protein: 15.5 g | Sodium: 287 mg
Fiber: 10.3 g | Carbohydrates: 55.2 g | Sugar: 4.9 g

Cheesy Quinoa Broccoli Casserole

Quinoa and broccoli aren't the most appetizing foods to many people, but they're both so full of nutritional benefits, it's worth including them in your diet. To make them more appetizing, consider cooking them into a casserole like this one, which is filled with garlic, onion, Cheddar, and mozzarella. This dish is healthy too! In addition to the protein from the quinoa and the broccoli, there's a little sprinkle of hemp seeds and flaxseed meal on top with the bread crumbs for extra nutrients.

Serves 8

Recipe Prep Time: *20 minutes*
Recipe Cook Time: *55 minutes*

2 cups quinoa

4 cups low-sodium vegetable broth

2 cups chopped broccoli florets

1 tablespoon extra-virgin olive oil

1 large yellow onion, peeled and chopped

2 large cloves garlic, peeled and finely chopped

1 cup unsweetened almond milk

¼ teaspoon salt

¼ teaspoon black pepper

½ cup shredded Cheddar cheese

3 tablespoons hemp seeds

1 tablespoon flaxseed meal

1 tablespoon bread crumbs

½ cup shredded mozzarella cheese

1 Preheat oven to 375°F. Grease a 9" × 13" baking dish with cooking spray.

2 Add quinoa and vegetable broth to a large saucepan and bring to a boil. Reduce to a simmer, cover, and cook until all the liquid is absorbed, about 20–25 minutes. During the last 5 minutes, add broccoli florets and cover the pot again, letting the broccoli steam until softened.

3 While quinoa is cooking, add olive oil to a large pan on medium heat. Add onion and garlic, and cook 4–5 minutes until onions are translucent. Reduce heat to medium-low and add almond milk, salt, and pepper; mix to combine. Bring to a light simmer, and remove from heat.

4 Add the quinoa and broccoli to the baking dish along with the contents of the almond milk pan and Cheddar. Mix together and spread evenly in the baking dish. In a small bowl, combine hemp seeds, flaxseed meal, and bread crumbs. Sprinkle on mozzarella and top with the bread crumb mixture. Bake 25–30 minutes until cheese starts to get crispy around the edge.

Per Serving

Calories: 276 | Fat: 9.9 g | Protein: 12.0 g | Sodium: 270 mg
Fiber: 4.7 g | Carbohydrates: 33.4 g | Sugar: 2.2 g

CHAPTER 10

DESSERTS AND SWEETS

Chocolate Peanut Butter Cups

If you love eating peanut butter cups, you'll love these plant-protein-packed treats. With this recipe, you can make your own, healthier version of the store-bought favorite using just coconut oil, cocoa powder, pure maple syrup, and peanut butter. These cups are best stored frozen, but you can eat them cold, or let them cool a little before indulging.

Makes 6 cups

Recipe Prep Time: *35 minutes*
Recipe Cook Time: *N/A*

6 tablespoons melted coconut oil
6 tablespoons unsweetened cocoa powder
1 tablespoon pure maple syrup
6 tablespoons raw creamy peanut butter

1 Combine melted coconut oil, cocoa powder, and maple syrup in a medium bowl until smooth. Line a 6-cup muffin tin with cupcake foils. Spoon half the mixture evenly into the 6 cups. Transfer to the freezer until chocolate hardens, about 15 minutes.

2 Remove from the freezer and spoon 1 tablespoon peanut butter into each chocolate cup. Cover with remaining melted chocolate. Make sure peanut butter is completely covered with chocolate. Freeze 20 minutes or until chocolate is hard. Keep frozen up to 3 months.

Per 1 cup

Calories: 233 | Fat: 21.5 g | Protein: 5.1 g | Sodium: 1 mg
Fiber: 3.5 g | Carbohydrates: 8.9 g | Sugar: 3.1 g

SWITCH UP THE FILLING

Once you know how to make these cups, you can mess around with what goes in the middle. Try using almond butter, blended dates, or coconut butter.

Almond Butter Oatmeal Cookies

Instead of making traditional cookies with flour and sugar, why not get some nutrients out of your dessert by making cookies with almond butter and oats instead? These Almond Butter Oatmeal Cookies are crisp on the outside and chewy on the inside, and they only require a few ingredients. They're also dairy-free and vegan-friendly, as they use flaxseed meal as a binder instead of eggs.

Makes 1 dozen cookies

Recipe Prep Time: *10 minutes*
Recipe Cook Time: *20 minutes*

1 tablespoon flaxseed meal
3 tablespoons water
1½ cups rolled oats
1 cup unsalted raw creamy
   almond butter
½ cup pure maple syrup
½ teaspoon pure vanilla
   extract
¼ teaspoon ground
   cinnamon

1   Preheat oven to 350°F. Line a 10" × 15" baking sheet with parchment paper.

2   In a small bowl, combine flaxseed meal and water and stir. Let sit 5 minutes to thicken.

3   In a large bowl, combine oats, almond butter, maple syrup, vanilla, and cinnamon. Stir in flaxseed meal mixture.

4   Roll dough into 2" balls; place on prepared baking sheet, lightly pressing down on each ball with a fork to flatten. Bake 20 minutes or until cookies start to firm up and are golden brown.

Per 1 cookie

Calories: 195 | Fat: 11.6 g | Protein: 6.1 g | Sodium: 1 mg
Fiber: 3.8 g | Carbohydrates: 19.8 g | Sugar: 9.5 g

Fig and Strawberry Crumble

It's hard to find fruity desserts that contain protein, but this crumble does just that. Although it's not as loaded with protein as desserts that contain nuts, beans, or legumes, this crumble does have some protein thanks to the almond flour and oats. And if you don't like figs, feel free to experiment and top the dessert off with a different fruit, like bananas or apples.

Serves 4

Recipe Prep Time: *10 minutes*
Recipe Cook Time: *30 minutes*

Filling

4 cups trimmed and chopped strawberries

1 tablespoon almond flour

2 teaspoons pure vanilla extract

Juice and zest of 1 small lemon

1 tablespoon pure maple syrup

Crumble

¾ cup almond flour

½ cup rolled oats

¼ cup melted coconut oil

2 tablespoons coconut sugar

1 tablespoon pure maple syrup

6 figs, halved

1 Preheat oven to 350°F. Grease an 8" × 8" or 6" × 10" baking dish with cooking spray.

2 **For Filling:** Add all filling ingredients to a medium bowl and mix well. Spoon mixture into baking dish.

3 **For Crumble:** In a separate medium bowl, combine flour, oats, coconut oil, coconut sugar, and maple syrup. Mix until crumbly. Spoon the crumble over strawberry mixture.

4 Place figs on top of crumble. Bake 25–30 minutes until top is crispy and strawberries are bubbling. Let cool 15 minutes, then serve.

Per Serving

Calories: 432 | Fat: 23.1 g | Protein: 3.0 g | Sodium: 3 mg
Fiber: 9.1 g | Carbohydrates: 52.8 g | Sugar: 33.4 g

Black Bean Brownies

You may be hesitant to try these Black Bean Brownies, but you'll be so surprised at the way this fudgy dessert tastes that you won't even realize that they contain beans. The black beans blend together with the cocoa powder and coconut sugar to create a chocolatey brownie that's both vegan and gluten-free (as long as you get dairy-free chocolate chips). If you want them to be a bit healthier, you can cut out the chocolate chips altogether, or you can replace them with cacao nibs to give these brownies a little crunch.

Makes 12 brownies

Recipe Prep Time: *20 minutes*
Recipe Cook Time: *30 minutes*

¼ cup plus 1 teaspoon melted coconut oil, divided

3 tablespoons warm water

2 tablespoons flaxseed meal

1 (15-ounce) can unsalted black beans, rinsed and drained

¼ cup almond flour

¼ cup unsweetened cocoa powder

½ cup coconut sugar

1 teaspoon pure vanilla extract

¼ teaspoon sea salt

1 teaspoon baking powder

¼ cup semisweet chocolate chips

1 Preheat oven to 350°F. Grease an 8" × 8" baking dish with 1 teaspoon coconut oil. Prepare the flaxseed "egg" by adding water and flaxseed to a small bowl. Stir and let sit for 15 minutes until flaxseeds are gummy.

2 Add all the ingredients, except the chocolate chips, to a blender or food processor, and blend on high until the mixture is smooth, about a minute or so.

3 Spoon the batter evenly into the pan. Bake 20–30 minutes until the outside begins to get crisp. Let cool 15 minutes to set. Brownies will be chewy, but will become firmer as they set. Store in the refrigerator to keep longer.

Per 1 brownie

Calories: 146 | Fat: 7.3 g | Protein: 2.9 g | Sodium: 138 mg
Fiber: 3.8 g | Carbohydrates: 18.6 g | Sugar: 10.6 g

··

SALT IN BLACK BEANS

To avoid making these brownies unnecessarily salty, be sure to buy low- or no-sodium black beans. Or, make your own using dried beans at home, and just don't add salt.

··

Almond Butter Fudge

Let's be honest: fudge is delicious! Luckily, this clean-eating fudge made with just almond butter and coconut oil doesn't contain any dairy or refined sugar. The almond butter used in this recipe provides protein, and the maple syrup adds some sweetness to this rich—but light—dessert. And if you're a fan of nutty fudge, feel free to use crunchy almond butter instead of creamy.

Makes 9 squares

Recipe Prep Time: *2 hours 10 minutes*
Recipe Cook Time: *N/A*

¾ cup raw creamy almond butter
¼ cup melted coconut oil
½ cup unsweetened cocoa powder
¼ cup pure maple syrup
¼ teaspoon sea salt

1 Line an 8" × 8" baking dish with parchment paper. In a large bowl, mix together almond butter, coconut oil, cocoa, maple syrup, and sea salt until smooth.

2 Spread evenly into the prepared dish and freeze at least 2 hours. Cut into squares and keep frozen.

Per 1 square

Calories: 205 | Fat: 17.0 g | Protein: 5.6 g | Sodium: 66 mg
Fiber: 4.4 g | Carbohydrates: 12.6 g | Sugar: 6.7 g

Chickpea Cookie Dough

Eating cookie dough out of the bowl is definitely a guilty pleasure, but it's not exactly the healthiest choice. But with this Chickpea Cookie Dough, you can grab a spoon and eat this up without any regrets! You'll never believe it, but this cookie dough is made with just chickpeas and peanut butter—no butter, eggs, or sugar needed—so nibble on it guilt-free.

Serves 6

Recipe Prep Time: *15 minutes*
Recipe Cook Time: *N/A*

- 1 (15-ounce) can chickpeas, rinsed and drained
- ½ cup raw creamy peanut butter
- 1 tablespoon pure maple syrup
- ½ teaspoon pure vanilla extract
- ⅛ teaspoon sea salt
- ¾ cup dark chocolate chips

Combine chickpeas, peanut butter, maple syrup, vanilla, and sea salt in a blender or food processor and blend on high until smooth, about 20–30 seconds. Add to a bowl, and mix in chocolate chips. Keep refrigerated up to 3 days.

Per Serving

Calories: 354 | Fat: 21.4 g | Protein: 9.1 g | Sodium: 138 mg
Fiber: 6.7 g | Carbohydrates: 32.6 g | Sugar: 17.1 g

DON'T TRY TO MAKE THESE INTO COOKIES

As delicious as this Chickpea Cookie Dough tastes, it unfortunately can't be baked into cookies, as this recipe is formulated to just be enjoyed "raw." If you try to bake this dough, you'll see that it won't expand or rise the way you want it to.

Peanut Butter Bliss Balls

If you're someone who likes just a bite of dessert, you'll love these peanut butter bliss balls. These indulgent bite-sized treats are filled with nutrient-rich ingredients, and better yet, they're all-natural, so you can even pop one in your mouth before heading out the door in the morning. After all, no one ever said you can't have dessert for breakfast!

Makes 12 balls

Recipe Prep Time: *50 minutes*
Recipe Cook Time: *N/A*

1 cup pitted Medjool dates
3 tablespoons raw creamy
   peanut butter
2 tablespoons unsweetened
   cocoa powder
2 tablespoons unsweetened
   shredded coconut
1 tablespoon chia seeds

1 Soak dates in hot water 30 minutes to soften. Drain the water from the dates, and add the dates to a blender or food processor along with peanut butter, cocoa powder, and shredded coconut; blend on high speed until a paste forms, about 20–30 seconds.

2 Add the chia seeds to a bowl. Roll the paste into 1" balls and then roll each ball through the chia seeds to coat. Refrigerate 15 minutes to set. Keep refrigerated in an airtight container. Bliss balls will keep up to a week.

Per 1 ball

Calories: 78 | Fat: 2.8 g | Protein: 1.7 g | Sodium: 0 mg
Fiber: 2.2 g | Carbohydrates:13.9 g | Sugar: 10.9 g

White Bean Blondies

Traditional blondies are like brownies, but they're made with vanilla instead of chocolate. Just like you can use black beans to make brownies in the Black Bean Brownies recipe earlier in this chapter, you can use white beans to make blondies here. But these blondies are so delicious that you would never know they're made primarily of beans. In addition to giving you a sense of indulgence, these blondies are filled with protein, thanks to the cannellini beans, peanut butter, and oat flour, and they are gluten-free, refined sugar–free, and dairy-free. If you're vegan, just make sure to opt for dairy-free chocolate chips.

Makes 9 blondies

Recipe Prep Time: *15 minutes*
Recipe Cook Time: *30 minutes*

1½ cups canned cannellini beans (rinsed and drained)

¼ cup raw creamy peanut butter

2 tablespoons melted coconut oil

1 tablespoon pure vanilla extract

½ cup oat flour (rolled oats ground into flour)

1 cup coconut sugar

½ teaspoon baking powder

½ teaspoon salt

½ cup dark chocolate chips

1 Preheat oven to 350°F. Lightly grease an 8" × 8" baking dish with cooking spray.

2 In a blender or food processor, blend together white beans, peanut butter, coconut oil, and vanilla on high speed until mixture is smooth, about 20–30 seconds. Transfer to a large bowl.

3 In a small bowl, combine oat flour, coconut sugar, baking powder, and salt. Add the dry mixture to the wet mixture and mix together evenly. Then mix in the chocolate chips.

4 Pour the batter into the baking dish, and bake 20–30 minutes until the top of the blondies are golden and start to crack. Let cool before slicing.

Per 1 blondie

Calories: 287 | Fat: 11.4 g | Protein: 5.5 g | Sodium: 157 mg
Fiber: 3.8 g | Carbohydrates: 41.7 g | Sugar: 28.3 g

Strawberry Chia Cheesecake Bars

Certain foods blow your mind the first time you ever try them, and this dessert is one of those foods. These cheesecake bars are completely vegan, as the crust is made with just pecans and dates, the filling with cashews and coconut cream, and the top layer with strawberries and chia seeds. It's hard to imagine the amazing creaminess of these fruity bars until you take a bite for yourself, but once you start nibbling on them, you might not want to stop—and nobody will tell you that you have to!

Makes 12 bars

Recipe Prep Time: *8 hours*
Recipe Cook Time: *N/A*

Crust

1 cup chopped raw pecans
½ cup Medjool dates, pits removed
¼ teaspoon salt

Filling

1½ cups raw unsalted cashews
½ cup room temperature full-fat coconut cream
½ cup plus 2 tablespoons pure maple syrup, divided
¼ cup melted coconut oil
2 teaspoons pure vanilla extract
2 tablespoons lemon juice
1 cup whole frozen strawberries
3 tablespoons water
¼ cup chia seeds

1 **For Crust:** Line an 8" × 8" baking pan with parchment paper. In a food processor or blender, combine pecans, dates, and salt and blend on high speed for about 10–15 seconds. Mixture should be combined, but still have a coarse texture.

2 Add the mixture to the baking pan and press down to make the crust. Stick in the refrigerator to set while you make your filling.

3 **For Filing:** Add the cashews to a large bowl and cover in boiling water. Let sit 1 hour to soften.

4 In a high-speed blender, blend together cashews, coconut cream, ½ cup maple syrup, melted coconut oil, vanilla, and lemon juice until smooth. Remove the crust from the refrigerator and pour the filling on top, smoothing the top so it's even. Return to the refrigerator.

5 Add the strawberries, 2 tablespoons maple syrup, water, and chia seeds to a blender or food processor and blend on high speed until smooth, about 10–20 seconds. Pour the mixture on top of the cheesecake layer. Freeze at least 3 hours or overnight. To serve, let thaw 20 minutes, and then cut into squares.

Per 1 bar

Calories: 313 | Fat: 21.8 g | Protein: 5.0 g | Sodium: 54 mg
Fiber: 3.4 g | Carbohydrates: 27.1 g | Sugar: 17.8 g

Chickpea Chocolate Truffles

Take one bite of these chewy chocolatey truffles, and you'll find yourself craving this dessert over and over again. Since all you can taste is chocolate, you'll be shocked to find these truffles are made with mostly chickpeas! The chickpeas, along with the almond butter, almond flour, and walnuts, add a huge amount of plant-based protein to this dish…and these truffles are much lower in sugar than your traditional chocolate truffle, which will save you from that sugar crash later in the day.

Makes 12 truffles

Recipe Prep Time: *1 hour 30 minutes*
Recipe Cook Time: *N/A*

- ¾ cup canned chickpeas (rinsed and drained)
- ¾ cup raw creamy almond butter
- 3 tablespoons pure maple syrup
- 2 tablespoons unsweetened cocoa powder
- ⅓ cup almond flour
- ½ cup dark chocolate chips
- 2 tablespoons crushed raw walnuts
- ½ teaspoon sea salt

1 In a food processor or blender, blend together chickpeas on high speed until smooth, about 10–20 seconds. Add almond butter, maple syrup, cocoa powder, and almond flour and blend on high until it forms a dough-like consistency, another 10–20 seconds.

2 Line a 10" × 15" baking sheet with parchment paper. Roll the dough into 1½" balls. Place the balls evenly on the baking sheet, and transfer to the refrigerator for 15 minutes.

3 While balls are in the fridge, melt the chocolate chips in a microwave-safe bowl 30 seconds at a time until fully melted, stirring in between each heating.

4 Dip each ball into the chocolate, coating it almost completely, and place back on the baking sheet. Top with a little bit of walnuts and sea salt.

5 Return baking sheet to the refrigerator and let sit at least 1 hour. Keep in an airtight container in the refrigerator to store. Truffles will last up to 5 days.

Per 1 truffle

Calories: 194 | Fat: 13.6 g | Protein: 4.8 g | Sodium: 117 mg
Fiber: 4.0 g | Carbohydrates: 15.2 g | Sugar: 8.5 g

Coconut Brown Rice Pudding

Since brown rice is a protein-rich grain, it's the perfect ingredient for a dessert. This brown rice pudding is completely dairy-free, as it's made with coconut milk instead of regular milk and butter. And, since no one cares if a dessert is healthy if it doesn't taste good, the cinnamon and coconut give this dish a flavor that you have to try to believe.

Serves 6

Recipe Prep Time: *10 minutes*
Recipe Cook Time: *35 minutes*

2½ cups water
1 cup uncooked brown rice
1½ cups canned coconut milk
¼ teaspoon ground cinnamon
¼ teaspoon ground cardamom
3 tablespoons coconut sugar
¼ cup unsweetened shredded coconut
½ cup sliced almonds

1 Bring water and rice to a boil in a medium pot. Reduce to a simmer, cover, and cook 30 minutes.

2 When rice is finished cooking, heat coconut milk over medium heat in a separate medium pot. Stir in cinnamon, cardamom, and coconut sugar, and reduce to a simmer.

3 Add rice and stir. Let simmer 3–5 minutes until most of the liquid is absorbed, stirring frequently. Mix in coconut and sliced almonds. Serve warm.

Per Serving

Calories: 474 | Fat: 27.0 g | Protein: 8.1 g | Sodium: 14 mg
Fiber: 3.8 g | Carbohydrates: 52.0 g | Sugar: 10.3 g

Raspberry Banana Soft Serve with Almonds

You won't believe it when you taste how amazing this dessert is, but this nondairy soft serve is made with just fruit and almond milk. While that's amazing enough on its own, this recipe adds almonds and protein powder to create the ultimate guilt-free treat--especially on hot days. If you would rather not have raspberry, you can use any other berry or fruit instead to switch up the flavor.

Serves 4

Recipe Prep Time: *15 minutes*
Recipe Cook Time: *N/A*

4 frozen bananas, peeled and sliced

1 cup frozen raspberries, plus 1 tablespoon extra for toppings

¼ cup Ginger Pea Protein Powder (Chapter 1)

½ teaspoon pure vanilla extract

½ cup unsweetened almond milk

¼ cup sliced raw almonds

1 In a blender or food processor, blend together bananas, 1 cup raspberries, protein powder, vanilla, and almond milk on high speed until evenly combined and smooth, about 20–30 seconds.

2 Use an ice cream scooper to scoop out the soft serve into a bowl. Top with almonds and remaining 1 tablespoon raspberries.

Per Serving

Calories: 215 | Fat: 4.6 g | Protein: 9.7 g | Sodium: 23 mg
Fiber: 7.1 g | Carbohydrates: 34.2 g | Sugar: 16.4 g

HIGH-SPEED BLENDER

To get the best results for this soft serve, you'll want to use a high-speed blender or food processor. Since the bananas have to be blended when they're frozen, a lower power machine won't work as well.

Banana Bread

There's nothing like banana bread to make you feel at home. But this updated Banana Bread recipe is vegan, gluten-free, and refined sugar–free. Be sure to use ripe bananas when making this dish. They'll make sure the bread is moist and add a sweeter flavor than green or yellow bananas. You can make variations of this Banana Bread by mixing in other ingredients in addition to walnuts, including dried fruit, chocolate chips, and other types of nuts or seeds.

Serves 8

Recipe Prep Time: *15 minutes*
Recipe Cook Time: *45 minutes*

3 medium ripe bananas, plus 1 peeled and sliced banana for topping

¼ cup melted coconut oil

¼ cup unsweetened almond milk

1 teaspoon pure vanilla extract

1½ cups almond flour

½ cup "From Scratch" Protein Powder (Chapter 1)

½ cup coconut sugar

1 teaspoon ground cinnamon

½ teaspoon baking soda

1 teaspoon baking powder

½ teaspoon salt

¼ cup chopped raw walnuts

1 Preheat oven to 350°F. Spray a 9" × 5" loaf pan with nonstick spray.

2 In a large bowl, mash 3 bananas with a fork, leaving them a little bit chunky. Add coconut oil, almond milk, and vanilla, and stir until combined.

3 In a medium bowl, combine almond flour, protein powder, coconut sugar, cinnamon, baking soda, baking powder, and salt. Fold the dry mixture into the wet mixture until evenly combined. Then fold in walnuts.

4 Transfer the batter to the pan and top with remaining sliced banana. Bake 45 minutes to 1 hour until top is firm and comes out mostly clean with a toothpick. Let cool before cutting into slices.

Per Serving

Calories: 359 | Fat: 22.3 g | Protein: 4.4 g | Sodium: 290 mg
Fiber: 6.5 g | Carbohydrates: 34.5 g | Sugar: 20.0 g

Chocolate Hazelnut Cookies

These protein-filled Chocolate Hazelnut Cookies are inspired by Nutella—but they don't use the packaged product. Instead, they use homemade hazelnut spread that's packed with fresh-roasted hazelnuts, cocoa powder, and maple syrup. You can even make extra and use the spread on top of your cookies or you can give in and eat it with a spoon.

Makes 12 cookies

Recipe Prep Time: *20 minutes*
Recipe Cook Time: *25 minutes*

1 cup raw hazelnuts
¼ cup coconut oil
¼ cup unsweetened cocoa powder
2 tablespoons pure maple syrup
2 tablespoons unsweetened almond milk
1 cup rolled oats
2 tablespoons flaxseed meal

1   Preheat oven to 350°F. Spread hazelnuts on a medium baking sheet and roast about 10 minutes. Let cool. Remove skin from the nuts that peel off easily (don't worry about the rest). Blend hazelnuts in a blender or food processor on high speed until hazelnuts turn into a butter, about 5 minutes. Scrape the side of the blender for best results.

2   In a small saucepan, heat coconut oil over medium-low heat. Add cocoa powder and maple syrup, stirring until a chocolate syrup forms. Add hazelnut butter and mix together.

3   In a medium bowl, combine chocolate hazelnut spread with almond milk, oats, and flaxseed meal. Using your hands, form the batter into 2" balls. Place on a baking sheet and press flat. Bake 15 minutes; let cool slightly before eating. Top each cookie with a spoonful of extra Nutella, if desired.

Per 1 cookie

Calories: 153 | Fat: 11.9 g | Protein: 3.1 g | Sodium: 2 mg
Fiber: 2.7 g | Carbohydrates: 10.0 g | Sugar: 2.7 g

Pumpkin Seed Bark

Bark is an easy dessert that everyone can make, no matter your baking skills. For this fall-inspired dish, you need some quality dark chocolate to melt, some raw pumpkin seeds, and sea salt, and you have a sweet and salty treat that also doubles as a nice afternoon snack. Close your eyes when you eat it and you can practically feel the crisp autumn air!

Serves 8

Recipe Prep Time: *1 hour 15 minutes*
Recipe Cook Time: *2 minutes*

½ pound dark chocolate
  (70% or higher cocoa)
½ cup raw pumpkin seeds
¼ teaspoon sea salt

1 Break chocolate into chunks. Melt chocolate by putting the chunks in a microwave-safe bowl and microwaving in 30-second increments, stirring after each time so the chocolate doesn't burn. Repeat until chocolate is melted, about 2 minutes.

2 Stir the pumpkin seeds into the chocolate. Spread a 10" × 15" baking sheet with parchment paper, and pour the chocolate mixture onto the parchment paper in an even layer using a rubber spatula, about ⅓" thick.

3 Top with sea salt, and then let cool to room temperature. Refrigerate to set about 1 hour. To serve, break into pieces. Store in an airtight container in the refrigerator.

Per Serving

Calories: 214 | Fat: 14.6 g | Protein: 4.7 g | Sodium: 78 mg
Fiber: 3.6 g | Carbohydrates: 13.9 g | Sugar: 6.9 g

Chocolate Chip Walnut Cookies

Everyone loves chocolate chip cookies, and this vegan and gluten-free twist on this favorite uses protein powder to give it an extra boost. These nutty cookies are light, fluffy, and a little crumbly, and they can be made in just over 30 minutes, which makes them perfect for the days you feel like baking on a whim, especially because you'll likely already have all of the ingredients on hand.

Makes 12 cookies

Recipe Prep Time: *20 minutes*
Recipe Cook Time: *15 minutes*

1 tablespoon flaxseed meal
3 tablespoons warm water
½ cup Chocolate Cinnamon Brown Rice Protein Powder (Chapter 1)
1 cup almond flour
1 teaspoon baking powder
½ cup peanut butter
¼ cup melted coconut oil
2 tablespoons crushed walnuts
⅓ cup semi-sweet chocolate chips (opt for dairy-free if vegan)

1 Preheat oven to 350°F. Line a 10" × 15" baking sheet with parchment paper.

2 Prepare flaxseed "egg" by combining flaxseed meal and warm water in a small bowl. Let sit 15 minutes.

3 In a large bowl, combine protein powder, almond flour, and baking powder.

4 In a separate medium bowl, combine peanut butter, coconut oil, and flaxseed egg.

5 Mix the wet ingredients into the dry ingredients, then fold in walnuts and chocolate chips. Form dough into 2" balls, and lightly press on the top to slightly flatten. Bake 12–15 minutes until cookies turn golden on the outside. Let cool before serving.

Per 1 cookie

Calories: 191 | Fat: 16.5 g | Protein: 4.3 g | Sodium: 42 mg
Fiber: 2.9 g | Carbohydrates: 7.0 g | Sugar: 1.8 g

Sticky Dark Chocolate Pistachio Bars

These clean-eating pistachio bars are filled with all the goods, including nuts, seeds, and oats, making them a protein powerhouse. The base of this dessert is made with dates, almond butter, tahini, and cocoa powder, and some dark chocolate is also melted and drizzled on top. These decadent bars are meant to be sticky, but the longer you refrigerate them, the more firm they'll get.

Makes 9 bars

Recipe Prep Time: *4 hours*
Recipe Cook Time: *2 minutes*

1 cup pitted Medjool dates
2 tablespoons raw almond butter
1 tablespoon tahini
1 tablespoon unsweetened cocoa powder
¼ cup pure maple syrup
½ cup rolled oats
2 tablespoons chia seeds
2 tablespoons hemp seeds
½ cup pistachio meats, plus 1 teaspoon crushed pistachios
½ cup chopped dark chocolate (70% or higher cocoa)

1 Blend together dates, almond butter, tahini, cocoa powder, and maple syrup in a food processor or blender on high speed until a smooth paste forms, about 1–2 minutes. Transfer to a large bowl.

2 Mix in oats, chia seeds, hemp seeds, and pistachios. Line an 8" × 8" baking dish with parchment paper, and spread the mixture evenly into the dish. Press down flat with a spatula or the back of a spoon.

3 Add dark chocolate to a medium microwave-safe bowl. Microwave on high in 30-second increments until melted (about 1–2 minutes total depending on your microwave's wattage).

4 Drizzle the chocolate over the bars. Refrigerate 3–4 hours to set. Cut into squares. Keep refrigerated up to 1 week.

Per 1 bar

Calories: 264 | Fat: 12.2 g | Protein: 5.2 g | Sodium: 3 mg
Fiber: 5.1 g | Carbohydrates: 36.5 g | Sugar: 25.7 g

Appendix: US/Metric Conversion Chart

VOLUME CONVERSIONS

US Volume Measure	Metric Equivalent
⅛ teaspoon	0.5 milliliter
¼ teaspoon	1 milliliter
½ teaspoon	2 milliliters
1 teaspoon	5 milliliters
½ tablespoon	7 milliliters
1 tablespoon (3 teaspoons)	15 milliliters
2 tablespoons (1 fluid ounce)	30 milliliters
¼ cup (4 tablespoons)	60 milliliters
⅓ cup	90 milliliters
½ cup (4 fluid ounces)	125 milliliters
⅔ cup	160 milliliters
¾ cup (6 fluid ounces)	180 milliliters
1 cup (16 tablespoons)	250 milliliters
1 pint (2 cups)	500 milliliters
1 quart (4 cups)	1 liter (about)

WEIGHT CONVERSIONS

US Weight Measure	Metric Equivalent
½ ounce	15 grams
1 ounce	30 grams
2 ounces	60 grams
3 ounces	85 grams
¼ pound (4 ounces)	115 grams
½ pound (8 ounces)	225 grams
¾ pound (12 ounces)	340 grams
1 pound (16 ounces)	454 grams

OVEN TEMPERATURE CONVERSIONS

Degrees Fahrenheit	Degrees Celsius
200 degrees F	95 degrees C
250 degrees F	120 degrees C
275 degrees F	135 degrees C
300 degrees F	150 degrees C
325 degrees F	160 degrees C
350 degrees F	180 degrees C
375 degrees F	190 degrees C
400 degrees F	205 degrees C
425 degrees F	220 degrees C
450 degrees F	230 degrees C

BAKING PAN SIZES

American	Metric
8 x 1½ inch round baking pan	20 x 4 cm cake tin
9 x 1½ inch round baking pan	23 x 3.5 cm cake tin
11 x 7 x 1½ inch baking pan	28 x 18 x 4 cm baking tin
13 x 9 x 2 inch baking pan	30 x 20 x 5 cm baking tin
2 quart rectangular baking dish	30 x 20 x 3 cm baking tin
15 x 10 x 2 inch baking pan	30 x 25 x 2 cm baking tin (Swiss roll tin)
9 inch pie plate	22 x 4 or 23 x 4 cm pie plate
7 or 8 inch springform pan	18 or 20 cm springform or loose bottom cake tin
9 x 5 x 3 inch loaf pan	23 x 13 x 7 cm or 2 lb narrow loaf or pate tin
1½ quart casserole	1.5 liter casserole
2 quart casserole	2 liter casserole

Index

Note: Page numbers in **bold** indicated recipe category table of contents. Page numbers in *italics* indicate photos.

About the Author

Carina Wolff is a health and wellness writer based in Santa Monica, California. She covers food, nutrition, and wellness for a variety of websites including *Bustle*, *Reader's Digest*, and *FabFitFun*. Additionally, she runs her own healthy food blog, *Kale Me Maybe*, where she creates plant-based clean-eating recipes. She is also the author of *The Spiralizer Recipe Book*. You can find more recipes on *Instagram*, @kalememaybe, or on Carina's blog at KaleMeMaybe.com.